Voyager
to
Destiny

Voyager
to
Destiny

The amazing adventures of Manjiro,
the man who changed worlds twice . . .

Emily V. Warinner

The Bobbs-Merrill Company, Inc.
Indianapolis - New York

Important Dates in the Life of Manjiro

(Gregorian Calendar)

1827 Born at Nakanohama village, Tosa province, Japan.

1841 Shipwrecked; rescued by New England whaler, *John Howland,* W. H. Whitfield, master; taken to Honolulu where his four companions remained.

1843 Arrived at Fairhaven, Massachusetts; given liberal education under the patronage of Captain Whitfield; enrolled in a private school before the establishment of public schools in America.

1846 Started extended whaling cruise in Atlantic and Pacific; became first mate; first Japanese to navigate a ship by Western scientific principles.

1849–1850 Prospected for gold in California. Prepared in Honolulu for return to Japan, for over two hundred years closed to returning voyagers and with but limited contact (through the Dutch) with the outside world; assisted by S. C. Damon, Seamen's Chaplain.

1851 Landed (January) on Ryukyu Island (Okinawa); sent on to Kagoshima, Japan; imprisoned; questioned; commanded to build a foreign ship; sent to Nagasaki; forced to trample on Christian symbols; imprisoned, minutely questioned concerning the Western world.

5

1852   (Latter half) Sent to home clan; imprisoned; questioned; allowed a brief visit with his mother; given low samurai status; became center of foreign culture.

1853   Called to Yedo (Tokyo) by Prime Minister following first visit of Commodore Perry; rank raised; consulted concerning the Americans.

1854   Translated official documents during Perry negotiations while guarded from contact with the Americans; in the service of the shipbuilding department of the Shogunate; teacher of English and things Western; allowed the unusual privilege of assuming surname; married; made curator of Western exhibits brought as gifts by Perry.

1856   Ordered to translate Bowditch's *New American Navigator,* first copy of which he brought to Japan.

1857   Instructor in naval training school; teacher of Western whaling methods; active in shipbuilding.

1859   Compiled a small book of conversational English.

1860   Accompanied as interpreter the first Japanese embassy to the United States; first Japanese to navigate a ship across the Pacific; visited his benefactor in Honolulu.

1861–1862   Member of whaling and colonizing expedition to Bonin Islands; returned with first foreign prisoner to be tried under extraterritoriality.

1863   More whaling.

1864   Called by the lord of Satsuma to become instructor in advanced naval methods.

1868–1869   Represented the Tosa clan in activities at the capital; made vice-principal of the school which became Tokyo Imperial University; resigned.

1870   Chosen to accompany a military delegation to Europe to observe the progress of the Franco-Prussian war; visited Captain Whitfield en route.

1872   Suffered a stroke of paralysis; recovered but forced to curtail active participation in government affairs.

1885   Chaplain S. C. Damon died February 7 at Honolulu.

1886   Letter from Marcellus Whitfield brought word of the death of Captain W. H. Whitfield, February 20, at Fairhaven.

1898   Manjiro died in Tokyo at the age of seventy-one.

On Manjiro's Name

THE problem of a consistent name for the character about whom this narrative revolves has been solved by the simple expedient of maintaining that by which he was known at the time of his shipwreck. Neither family name nor status was allowed commoners in Japan until after mid-nineteenth century. When in 1854, then twenty-seven years of age, Manjiro became Nakahama Manjiro (by long precedent the surname preceded the given name), he was perhaps the first to be so rewarded by his government. Nakahama was a shortened form of the name of his native village, so while the honor officially bestowed was an extraordinary one, he was literally Manjiro *of* Nakahama.

By American whalemen the young Japanese was known as John Mung, a name of which he was exceedingly proud, and by which he often signed himself.

When any of the three names appears in letters or other quotations they remain as written; otherwise I have used Manjiro exclusively.

E. V. W.

To the memory of my valiant Mother who, more than any other, shared in my quest for the elusive

Sow, simply sow the seed;
For as long as the year has its autumn
It will bear fruit—
If only the root survive—
Though the flower has withered.

UNKNOWN JAPANESE POET

Foreword

I CONSIDER it a highly valued privilege to write a foreword for Miss Warinner's fascinating story of Nakahama Manjiro. I believe in the importance of bringing to our people and the Japanese people such historical episodes as throw light on the traditional and now renewed friendship between our two countries. Her book admirably fulfills that purpose as well as that of an unusual adventure story.

The life of Manjiro is highly dramatic as well as significant of the inevitable trend of every people away from isolation. Through the extraordinary experience of his shipwreck and rescue, and the opportunity to learn English in the whaling town of Fairhaven, Massachusetts, before the establishment of a public-school system in America, Manjiro became an important link in opening up trade and official relations between our two countries. He was, indeed, the first Japanese to reach our country and to be educated there. For his remarkable service he deserves a prominent place in Japanese-American history. However belated, this recognition is right and fitting.

Miss Warinner shows an acute awareness of developments in Japan prior to and following Commodore Perry's demands and the push of the entire Western world, while disclaiming any attempt to record formal history. I hope her book will be widely read.

JOSEPH C. GREW

Author's Note

"Manjiro was a fabulous character of my boyhood," said the late President Franklin Delano Roosevelt to this writer. "My imagination conjured up a ragged fisherman who became a Prince. Now I think of his story as Americana. It should be better known. I wish you well in piecing it together."

Without such a challenge this story would never have been seriously attempted. For "piecing" has indeed been necessary, and the President himself had but a fragment to offer. His affection for the old whaling town of Fairhaven, Massachusetts, in which his great-grandfather had lived as successor to a pioneer settler, as a promoter of the whaling industry and clipper ship trade with China was apparent as he talked. It was from the venerable "Captain" Delano that the story of Manjiro, the shipwrecked Japanese, had come into the family, a story to be told and retold later by the President's grandfather. Warren Delano II had been in China at the time of the episode, but he relished the story as the first link with Japan, then closed to the world. To the boy, Franklin, it had always seemed a family tradition, though the rescue had been accomplished by W. H. Whitfield, a sea captain with ties no closer than those of other friendly villagers.

Most complete records of Manjiro in English are those left by the Reverend Samuel Chenery Damon, Seamen's Chaplain and editor of *The Friend*, "the oldest newspaper west of the Rockies," established in Honolulu in 1843. Mr. Damon was Manjiro's friend and mentor, who encouraged him as early as 1850 to make known to the people of his

15

homeland the friendly aims of the United States toward Japan, and who for the next thirty-four years followed his career with interest.

Records in Fairhaven and memories lingering there helped to round out the story on the American side.

In Japan, records have been scattered and incomplete, for fast-moving events after the arrival of Commodore Perry often obscured all but leading political figures, and the fisherman who had played a backstage part in treaty making was lost in the confusing tangle of history.

The discovery in 1912 of four seemingly related manuscripts displayed by secondhand bookdealers at the headquarters of the Tokyo Fine Arts Society, focused the attention of the late Mr. Stewart Culin, Curator of Ethnology at the Brooklyn Museum, upon what he instinctively felt was a collector's item. Although he was unable to read the Japanese text, he noticed sketches of New England scenes, evidently Japanese work, and was puzzled to know how the two could be associated.

Diligent inquiry revealed that he had uncovered the original story of Manjiro. Manjiro had told it himself on his return to Japan in 1852, when outside travel was strictly forbidden, and it was set down by an artist in his home province of Tosa on the island of Shikoku. The artist had copied his sketches from pictures brought home by Manjiro, or drawn them from Manjiro's descriptions. Where such descriptions had apparently baffled the artist, the narrator himself had supplied crude drawings signed "John Mung," the name given him by American seamen.

These original volumes were indeed a treasure, and Mr. Culin determined to use them to document the little-known story which he thought to write. Death cut short his plan, but through the great kindness of the museum authorities a typescript of a partial English translation was sent to this writer.

Fascinating as this translation is, phonetic spellings make portions undecipherable, and a mixture of lunar and Gregorian calendar dates adds to the confusion. Moreover, the abbreviated account deals chiefly with the period between Manjiro's shipwreck and his return to Japan some eleven years later. He had passed through the government trials at Nagasaki, which were mandatory for anyone who had left the home shores, yet information concerning them is scanty. Additional material was needed if anything like a comprehensive report of Manjiro's information on the West were to be given. Some of this was to be found in the original Japanese volumes which had been faithfully copied by Manjiro's son, the late Dr. Toichiro Nakahama, and members of his family while Mr. Culin remained in Tokyo. (Mr. Culin's report of his discovery and meeting with Dr. Nakahama appears in the Appendixes.) More facts were uncovered in the now exceedingly rare "newsletters" executed by hand at Nagasaki while Manjiro and his companions of the shipwreck were objects of curiosity and cautious speculation. Despite the government ban, information concerning the outside world was slowly disseminated by means of such writings, often loosely bound together in booklet form, and surreptitiously passed from hand to hand. Probably for the first time, these original records have now come to the attention of an American researcher.

In the upper left-hand corner of an attached letter, a memorandum, unsigned and undated, though clearly written by a person other than the original writer, gives the information: "I acquired these documents at Nagasaki under certain circumstances. They must be kept in secret because they deal with conditions in America, even speaking of which is prohibited by law."

Now treasured by collectors, these manuscript letters give information released at the trials which is obtainable nowhere else. At the time, the news was sensational. It was doubtless colored by individual interpretation, but certain facts stand out a century later as remarkably accurate.

Further evidence that information on the West was carefully guarded by the officials is in the foreword of a little mulberry paper book titled *Story of the Drifters,* hand-blocked at Nagasaki in 1852: "I recorded this for the purpose of distributing among my friends. It is kept in secret so I am prohibited to sell this book. Recorded by Dontsushi." (The name is undoubtedly a pseudonym.)

Somewhat later, bolder publications known as *Shimbun,* or Outlandish Stories, were hawked in the streets of Yedo (Tokyo) and caught the attention of the populace. Curiously, *shimbun* is the present-day term for newspaper, despite the high rating of the Fourth Estate in Japan.

Helpful as a guide throughout the study has been the biography, *Nakahama Manjiro den,* written in Japanese by Dr. Nakahama. Mr. Kiyoshi Nakahama, Manjiro's grandson, has been tireless as translator and interpreter.

Fulfilling his father's long-held wish, and with the cooperation of the Oriental Cultural Summer College, Mr. Nakahama and his family were hosts to Miss Allie Omey, a granddaughter of Captain Whitfield; Mrs. Thomas Whitfield, widow of the Captain's grandson; and her son, Mr. Willard Delano Whitfield, in Tokyo during the year 1940. The century-old friendship was widely acclaimed by the Japanese press and radio.

To Miss Ethel M. Damon, a granddaughter of the Reverend Samuel C. Damon, is due special gratitude for sustained interest and permission to examine family records. Without this help it would have been impossible to give due significance to Manjiro's story.

The keen interest of the Honorable Joseph C. Grew and Mrs. Grew has been most heartening, and to both I tender my thanks. Mrs. Grew is a great-grandniece of Commodore Perry.

For air transportation to Japan during the Perry Centennial in 1953, the United States Navy is gratefully remembered. Each of three previous visits had added its quota of background knowledge.

Acknowledgment is made to Dr. Shina Kan, of Tokyo Women's University, for intelligent help in revealing Japanese sources; to Dr. Sanki Ichikawa, professor emeritus of Tokyo University, and Mr. Frank Cary, American Board missionary in Japan, who told of the still-existing lesson chart used by Manjiro in his first English classes in Japan; and to Dr. Shigetoshi Kawatake, director of the Theatre Museum at Waseda University, who presented an original *ukiyo-e* depicting Manjiro as the hero of a *Kabuki* drama.

The assistance of Miss Naomi Fukuda, librarian at the International House of Japan; of Miss Avis Pillsbury of the Millicent Library at Fairhaven; and Miss Allie Omey is gratefully recalled. Thanks are also due to Mr. William H. Tripp, curator of the Old Dartmouth Historical Society and Whaling Museum; Mrs. Charles Hamlin, who contributed her memories of the commemorative celebration of 1918 in Fairhaven (see Appendixes); Miss Bernice Judd, who read the manuscript; and President Gregg Sinclair, who arranged for me to have assistance with translation at the University of Hawaii.

Sir George Sansom of Columbia University has been more than generous in granting permission to reproduce sketches of some of Manjiro's contemporaries from his authoritative *The Western World and Japan*. His book has also been of tremendous help in clarifying the conflicting period in which Japan, long isolated by choice, faced the necessity of submitting to Western pressure.

Although after his return home Manjiro often faced a blank wall of ignorance and hostility, Japanese leaders of necessity relied on him in an extraordinary crisis. His reports on the world he had seen at firsthand did not fall on sterile ground. For already within isolated Japan searching minds had sensed a wider compass. Such a mind had the celebrated Sakuma Shozan, who, despite early Confucian training, was to contribute to Japan's rebirth. In 1854, while in prison for conniving at an offense against the exclusion laws, Sakuma reflected:

> When I was twenty I knew that men were linked together in one province.
> When I was thirty I knew that they were linked together in one nation.
> When I was forty I knew that they were linked together in a world of five continents.
>
> EMILY V. WARINNER

Contents

Contents—continued

Picture Record of Manjiro's Two Worlds

EXCLUSION EDICT

1638-1855

Sending ships to foreign countries is strictly forbidden. He shall be put to death who secretly enters into a ship and is later detected. The captain of the ship shall be detained to wait for a decision from the Shogun. He shall be executed who went to a foreign country, staid there and later returned home. The reward of 200 or 300 pieces of silver according to the merits shall be given to one who has searched, detected and reported Christians. The descendants of southern barbarians [Portuguese and Spanish] shall be driven back to their own countries. If one shelter them he shall be dealt punishment and his relatives shall be punished according to the degree of the crime.

Voyager
to
Destiny

Prologue

WIND-SWEPT and solitary, Nakanohama village on the Japanese island of Shikoku faced the open sea. Clustered together, as if for mutual protection, the drab dwellings of the fisherfolk were low and thatched; floors were of beaten earth or cobblestones, windows of oiled paper. A low mat-covered platform raised the families above the floor drafts. Here above the chilly ground they all slept, ate and worked. Here the women sat to spin or weave, the men to patch or tinker. Bare of furniture, yet with the time-honored *tokonoma* (place of honor) for print or flower, it was the center of home life. Here folk tales were told and retold, village gossip related. Near at hand the ancestral record kept the dead within the circle of the living.

On the village common, against the sunset with its occasional flashes of misty gold, a group of pine trees leaned toward the sea. Gnarled and bent, they were revered for their age and pattern.

And as form and shadow delighted and refreshed the simple, nature-loving villagers, their very lives conformed to the pattern of the centuries. Without vision or hope of change, they lived within the narrow arc of the low-born.

So their fathers and grandfathers had lived before them. Fishermen, builders of boats, sail- and netmakers—all worked within prescribed limitations, each knowing the width of the groove in which circumstance had placed him, none dreaming of enlarging its sphere.

Against this background the boy Manjiro had been born. At fifteen years of age by Japanese reckoning, he had almost reached a man's estate. After the death of his father he was

29

regarded as head of the house, and was soon to be so registered, though the position traditionally belonged to his less vigorous elder brother. By the sign of the zodiac Manjiro had been born in the Year of the Wild Boar, a sure sign of courage. One name only he bore; no other was thought of or allowed, for his family possessed no *mon* or other distinguishing mark.

As sober-minded and hard-working as any youth in the village, Manjiro was yet different. Often overriding established ways and substituting those of his own, he was looked upon with mild disapproval—at best as a little queer—for no youth presumed to question. The latest story going the rounds was that when his neighbor set him to the task of polishing rice he had placed pebbles in the mortar to hasten the process.

Whoever had heard of such nonsense? If he kept on at this rate, he would come to no good end, said the elders. None could guess that this eager, inquisitive boy would one day tread new paths, paths that would lead to a world unknown. That high honors would come to him. That because of his services Japan would forge ahead as a great maritime nation. Strange twist of fate, incomprehensible.

1

Shipwreck

IT WAS January 5, 1841, the lucky Year of the Ox. In another two days rice gruel seasoned with the seven varieties of early herbs would be served throughout Japan as a fitting close to the Festival of the New Year.

Because of the seasonal demands supplies at Manjiro's home were already low. As the chief provider for his fatherless family, he felt his responsibility. He had welcomed the opportunity to join the experienced fisherman, Fudenojo, at Nishihama Usaura, a near-by village, and was now helping the last-minute preparations for the projected cruise.

Prospects were bright, for the much-prized sea bass came in great schools at this season. With favor from the gods the triumphal fishermen's song would herald their speedy return. Yet he suddenly began to feel remorse because, in his haste, he had not taken quite proper leave of his mother. There had been the usual *sayonara,* but that casual word of farewell often held a note of portent: *If it must be.* The thought lay like a shadow on his mind.

All morning Manjiro had carried water and fagots to the little twenty-four-foot fishing vessel anchored within wading distance of the shore. When the fishing started at sea, he would be the "unhooker," whose job was to remove fish

31

from the hooks and assist in emptying the nets, but now he was a general helper.

Fudenojo was busily engaged in laying in a supply of rice, charcoal and salt and making a final check of the nets. His other helpers were his brothers—Jusuke, aged twenty-five, and Goemon, sixteen— and his friend Toraemon, aged twenty-seven. Fudenojo himself was thirty-eight and the acknowledged leader. At fifteen Manjiro was the youngest.

Like all fishermen of the time, they would not venture far from the shore. Currents were strong, winds unpredictable. Built to government specifications, small boats used by fishermen and those in coastal commerce were open at the stern, easily swamped in the open sea. Larger craft belonging to the daimyo (feudal lords) were high at both ends with a raised pavilion in the center. Square sails increased their clumsiness.

Shrewd purpose lay behind their government-prescribed design. Intercourse with other parts of the world was forbidden by an exclusion edict in force for over two hundred years. Death for any who left the country and returned was the penalty, and timid navigation the result. "Contamination lies beyond the reach of the tides" had become a maxim never questioned.

After a hasty midday meal of rice, pickled turnip and tea, Fudenojo pronounced all in readiness and set his course for the nearest fishing grounds. The first day's catch was disheartening. At nightfall Fudenojo steered the boat behind a projecting shoulder of rock. They were quite alone now; other fishing craft had put into harbor. The second day passed with but scant success. Again at evening they sought shelter clear of the wind and lay at anchor through the night.

On the third day, after a school of mackerel and sea bream had brought them a plentiful catch, they suddenly became alarmed at the darkening sky. A twisting monkey-

and-cock wind warned them to take in their nets and head for shore.

As darkness fell and the storm increased, the peg of their sculling oar broke. Frantically they cut off a section of the gunwale and fastened the oar with straw rope. But the oar soon snapped, and the blade was swept instantly from sight.

Fudenojo at the helm fought hard, but the boat was beyond control. It flew like an arrow on the crest of mountainous waves. The wind shrieked and freezing spray swirled over them. Instinctively the five friends huddled together.

Sunrise brought new terror. They had drifted from Ashizuri Point across open water to Cape Muroto, a landmark for fishermen, and a lookout for ships in distress. But no signals appeared, and the helpless men knew that they were in deep trouble. Only prayers before their weather-beaten talisman could save them: *"Namu Amida Butsu . . . Namu Amida Butsu . . . Namu Amida Butsu* (Hail to the Eternal Splendor of Buddha).*" They intoned the words jerkily with deep feeling. Even Fudenojo's usually commanding voice was a supplication.

Came the next day, and the next. Their boat moved with a flowing rhythm now, and with horror they saw that the color of the water had changed. They were in the path of the *Kuro Shiwo,* the Black Current! The mountains of Kii gave them their last glimpse of Japan.

At noon on January 13, their eighth day at sea, they discovered a cluster of clouds on the distant horizon—or was it, perhaps, land? Birds flying a little distance away stirred their hopes.

The next day they could see the outlines of a tiny island. But the rocky coast line was forbidding. Questioned concerning their chances for a landing, Fudenojo shook his head. Oar, sails and rudder were gone. Though the tide was in their favor, the surf along the shore would surely wreck the boat and might be too strong for swimming. At an opportune moment, Fudenojo said, each man would have to strike out for himself.

An inborn sense of fatality seemed to foretell death. They no longer cared so much to reach a place of safety as to quench their thirst. The raw fish they had as food had only increased their need for water until now they were almost crazed with desire. There might be water on the island. To swim for it was their only hope.

Goemon, Manjiro and Toraemon leaped into the icy waves. Fudenojo and Jusuke were about to follow when the boat turned over on them. They were set free when the frame broke apart and floated away, but Jusuke's leg was injured.

Finally, bruised and bleeding, all crawled onto the rocks beyond the reach of the sea. It was long before the roar of the surf subsided; hours, it seemed, before they could hear one another. At length, prostrate, they passed into unconsciousness.

2

Torijima

WITH water their will to live revived. They found it in the crevices of the rocks and drank freely, unaware that times of no rain would bring acute suffering. For the present they could but rejoice at their deliverance.

The uninhabited island, Torijima* (Bird Island), proved to be slightly more than two miles in circumference. It seemed a great mass of rock hurled by a volcanic giant. At first the castaways could find no refuge. Finally they discovered a natural cave, small at the opening, yet large enough to offer a shelter to all of them. Driftwood from their foundered boat provided crude beds. It was of no use as fuel, since they had lost their flint and steel and could not strike fire.

For food they found *kaya,* the shoots of which they knew to be edible, and *gumi,* which in season yielded a small fruit. But the supply was dismayingly limited. Albatross were so tame at first that they alighted on their shoulders, but soon, apparently having learned a sense of danger, they flew higher and higher on the rocks. Manjiro became expert at knocking them down with rocks and skinning the

---

* Situated southeast of Honshu, the largest of the main Japanese group, little Torijima is in modern times the site of a government weather bureau.

flesh with no tool but a sharp piece of stone. To vary the monotony of their fare, he and his friends dried some of the meat, calling it "stone roast."

Soon birds' eggs, stringy and with a strong taste of fish, were added to the daily fare. But when the birds began to leave the island on their regular migration the men realized that they must depend on shellfish and occasional bits of seaweed found clinging to the rocks. If only enough water could be found, water, so plentiful in the rushing streams at home!

When it was almost gone, Fudenojo decreed that each man must limit himself to a small shellful of water after each meal. There must be no stealth, no cheating. Each one faithfully kept his pledge. To reduce the craving for water they learned to wipe off each bit of seaweed carefully before putting it into their mouths.

One day Manjiro and Fudenojo climbed to the highest point on the island and discovered an old well in which there was a small quantity of discolored water. Near by were two piles of stones, one surmounted by a crude monument. The two explorers decided these must be graves and marking them had probably been the last act of devotion by the surviving member of a shipwrecked crew. They experienced a certainty that they themselves would die, one by one. Manjiro thought often of his mother and sometimes softly called her name, knowing that she could not hear. "*Okāsan,* oh, *Okāsan! . . .*"

Near the end of a month they calculated to be April, a severe earthquake brought sudden terror. It was the end, they believed. But the shocks subsided, leaving a great pile of rocks obstructing the mouth of the cave. Frantically they pushed and strained until they had removed the debris and carried Jusuke into the sunlight.

They were worried about Jusuke. Often delirious, he seemed to see fireflies, and his companions remembered, with tightening throats, happy evenings in their homeland when whole families strolled out to watch the darting lights—moon-viewing nights, the ethereal beauty of spring blossoms. Cherry trees were perhaps blooming now, soon gone like other beautiful things. . . .

Manjiro had now taken over most of the job of providing food, since his health remained unimpaired and his aim was true. Just before sunrise one day in June, about the time of the new moon, he went alone to the shore. Neither he nor his companions ever failed to scan the horizon in the hope that a new day would bring relief. This morning Manjiro thought he could see a faint object far out at sea. Unwilling to be tricked by imagination and derided by the others—for not long before a ship had passed by at great distance—he waited, tensely watching.

When at length the speck had undoubtedly moved, Manjiro realized with a great gulp of emotion that it was indeed a ship. He rushed toward the cave from which Goemon and Toraemon had just emerged, pulled them toward the shore in an ecstasy of joy, and pointed toward the distant object.

Doubtful at first, his apathetic companions at length made out the outline of a strange ship. When after a time it appeared to turn in another direction, they avoided looking at one another, did not speak the fatalistic words *Shikata ga nai*, it can't be helped, so often heard from the lips of their elders. They knew that their chance of being saved was remote, but they were young and hope died hard. Because of their own disappointment they did not communicate the news to Fudenojo, who had not been well of late and spent most of his time with Jusuke in the cave.

Near noon the watchers saw the ship turn and lower what appeared to be small boats. "Rescuers!" cried the always hopeful Manjiro.

To a piece of driftwood they tied a ragged kimono and waved it in the breeze. Finally it caught the attention of the men in the boats. They had rowed in toward the island hoping to find a turtle to break their monotonous diet of salt meat and biscuit and had had no thought of landing. Now in answer to Manjiro's distress signal, they brought the boats within shouting distance. But their words were meaningless to the straining listeners on the shore. At length by gestures, they made known their willingness to take the castaways to the ship.

At close range the strangers—some wearing beards of different lengths and colors, and two with black skins— were a startling sight. The three Japanese had heard vaguely of "barbarians" from across the sea, the strange foreign devils of folk tales. These men in the boats must be such, but they smiled pleasantly and the sight of their ship shimmering in the sunlight promised rescue. The possibility of human help obliterated fear.

Manjiro and Goemon made their way over the rocks and scrambled aboard the nearest boat. Suddenly they remembered Fudenojo and Jusuke and began to gesture frantically toward the land.

Surmising that there were still others in the distressed group, two men went ashore and were led to the cave by Toraemon. When one bent over Fudenojo, he struggled upright to combat what seemed an evil form, as black as if painted with soot. Toraemon's shrill voice brought him to attention. When the situation had been made clear, the brothers accompanied their rescuers, Jusuke on his hands and knees. At the shore he plunged into the water and was pulled into the second boat.

Soon they were alongside the ship, a three-masted whaler of what seemed to the Japanese unbelievable proportions. Its rigging was strung like cobwebs in all directions. Its sails could not be counted. There was a flag of shining stars. Were they dreaming, and was it after all a phantom?

Manjiro put his palms together and knelt on the deck.

The sailors laughed, but he remained prostrate until touched on the shoulder and motioned to rise.

The captain's quarters seemed as impressive as a Buddhist temple, and the master was a person to be feared. He had, they thought, the features of a nobleman. When he spoke—and the Japanese could understand no word—there seemed a great gulf between them. Their simple greeting, *Konnichiwa,* was unanswered. Perhaps there was still no hope. . . .

The captain ordered clothing. The garments were new to them, with pipe-stem sleeves, in strange contrast to their flowing *kimono,* but warmed their shivering bodies. Someone brought steaming sweet potatoes and they began to eat ravenously. But very soon the captain ordered the food taken away. They did not understand and bowed their heads in disappointment. Long afterward they were to learn that starving men must be fed sparingly.

After a time they were given a kind of brown soup with very small pieces of animal food which they had never before tasted. It was delicious and satisfying. Later they were gratified to receive rice, their chief need. They soon learned to eat hardtack along with the crew. Of water they could not seem to get enough, for the ship's supply was necessarily limited.

In his logbook the captain had made the following entry:

SUNDAY, JUNE 27, 1841
This day light winds from S.E. Isle in sight 1 p.m. Sent in two boats to see if there was any turtle, found 5 poor distressed people on the isle, took them off, could not understand anything from them more than they was hungry. Made the latitude of the isle 30 deg. 31 m. N.

Unwilling to sail until he had given the castaways an opportunity to save their few possessions, the captain ordered a boat lowered the following morning. Manjiro, misunderstanding, threw himself at the captain's feet and begged not to be left behind. When the captain motioned him to get into the bobbing boat, he feared that he had been singled out for this fate. He could not bear the thought; sudden tears dimmed his eyes. As his friends stood with averted gaze, Fudenojo gave a low command and Manjiro climbed into the boat. To obey was instinctive, no matter what the cost. Happily, the boat soon returned, the smiling youth bearing a bundle of rags.

Sails were set, the anchor lifted. The breeze freshened. The ship began to move.

3

Deliverance

THE *John Howland,* Captain W. H. Whitfield, master, had sailed from the port of Fairhaven, Massachusetts, in 1839. The stout little ship of three hundred and seventy-nine tons, fitted out by the firm of James and John Howland, was bound for a whaling expedition in dangerous and unfriendly waters. It would cruise near Japan, a group of islands clearly charted but mysterious and forbidding. Luckless white men who had attempted to land there had been mistreated; some, according to reports, had been placed in cages and all but starved. Others had never been heard from. Clearly it was hands off—and hands off it would be for the crew of the *John Howland.* Whales were wanted, not trouble.

Now by a circuitous route the ship was bound for the Sandwich Islands where mail would be waiting. There, too, it would take on potatoes and fresh fruit. With careful planning the captain never had to worry about scurvy.

As the castaways had opportunity to explore the ship they discovered two shining cannon. There were also thirty rifles aboard. Thirty-four men made up the crew. Oil casks were everywhere.

In the hold the Japanese were amazed to find cows and

pigs carried for food. Thinking of the outcast *eta* of their own country, they supposed that the men who cared for the animals would be avoided, but they soon saw them at table with the others. Apparently they were on the same footing. Strange, oh, strange! So many things were strange! With a gradual acceptance of a life never even dreamed of, they learned not to fear.

The simple fishermen knew nothing of Japan's avid interest in a whaling industry apparently more advanced than their own, and did not suspect that appointed observers, using long-distance glasses of Dutch manufacture, were making every effort to gain a working knowledge of strange ships which came from parts unknown, only to disappear over the horizon. For this knowledge Japan would have to wait for more than a decade.

To the five waifs, familiar only with the ancient and hazardous method of snaring with nets, these new methods of killing monsters of the deep, of towing them to the ship, of cutting them up for the try-pots and storing the extracted oil were a revelation. They watched with a fascination akin to awe.

After he had been on the ship for several weeks Manjiro was one day given an opportunity to serve with the lookout. Perched in the crow's nest high in the rigging, he scrutinized the ocean in all directions. His "There she blows, blo-o-ws!" was shrill mimicry of the sailor's lusty shout, and produced the usual bustle of lowering boats. Everyone was excited, for the single spout sighted meant a sperm whale.

When the captured whale had been brought to the ship, the captain summoned Manjiro, praised his keen vision and presented him with a sailor's cap as reward. Gradually he and his companions were given regulation clothes. Shoes were their greatest problem. Manjiro, like the others, pre-

ferred bare feet, but kept his shoes at his side lest he be
without them when the captain signaled. He considered
them a mark of respect.

In the eyes of them all the captain rated this respect. Day
after day they had been impressed with the discipline on
the ship. Disobedience or negligence called forth an excla-
mation or bellow outlandish to Japanese ears, a straight
stern look of disapproval, and finally, after what seemed an
interminable period, a curt nod of dismissal. Had he been
put in irons, a miscreant could not have felt more crest-
fallen. After administering the rebuke the captain was his
own calm self again. Years later Manjiro could remember
no flogging on this ship.

Manjiro's knowledge of American words and ways increased rapidly as the voyage continued. The captain took
a personal interest in the boy's progress, often repeating a
difficult word, and later testing his memory. Just now he
was often saying "Ho-no-lulu," the name of a port in the
Sandwich Islands designated Fair Haven on early Pacific
maps. The captain was pleased with the thought, for the
words had their own meaning for him. Fairhaven, he tried
to explain, was his home port many thousand miles away
in a country called America.

Would Manjiro like to go there someday? he paused in
his pacing of the deck to ask. There he would see many ships
like the *John Howland*. In Honolulu, too, there would be
many vessels, for it was now perhaps the greatest whaling
port in the world. The year he had sailed, Fairhaven had
been rated the second largest.

Much of their communication was by signs, but the captain's hand on Manjiro's shoulder and his protégé's quick
intuition gave meaning to a flow of words otherwise unin-
telligible. It was as if the captain were saying. *You are a
good boy. I should like to help you. You can trust me.* And

pointing to the beckoning distance surely meant *Come with me into my world.*

Manjiro was fascinated. He tried to pass on his new knowledge to his friends. But they were slower of comprehension, not really interested.

4

Foreign Soil

IT WAS late November when the *John Howland* reached the port of Honolulu. For a day and two nights after the pilot had been signaled and was aboard, the ship tried to enter the inner harbor. "Wind out, could not get her in," noted Captain Whitfield in his log.

This experience was not uncommon, for vagaries of wind and tide had to be reckoned with, even on the lee side of the island. These were the days when ships, having crossed the outer harbor under their own sail, were then taken in tow by stalwart Hawaiians, sometimes four hundred strong. Bending brown backs to the rhythm of an ancient chant, they found it mere child's play to draw ships to safe anchorage. Fur traders who had in the past sought the harbor in great numbers had seen the ships moored so closely it was possible to step from the deck of one to that of another.

Even now, the harbor was a forest of masts! How enchanting the sight to the Japanese who, before their rescue, had never seen a foreign vessel at close range, or known the advantages of well-charted coasts.

Business between ship and shore would engage the captain's time for future weeks. Now, with his anchor down, his immediate business was to pick up his mail and make arrangements for the castaways.

Manjiro was never to forget his first confused impressions

of a foreign country. Closely following in the captain's steps, he and his friends found themselves in the midst of a clamoring crowd of dark-skinned people, with here and there a white man wearing clothes like the captain's. Some of the brown people wore only breechcloths—a not unfamiliar sight to the Japanese—while others appeared to be draped in paper. Women, mingling freely with the men, wore loose garments, with something on their heads called "bonnets."

Where, the Japanese must have wondered, were the flashing swords of haughty officials? Were there none to hold the crowd in check? Would not the people be punished for overstepping class bounds, for the impudence of laughingly casting a garland of flowers around the captain's neck? But he had laughed too, and seemed pleased.

Soon the captain shook hands with a number of white men, and they proceeded toward the village. The streets were ankle-deep in dust; two-wheeled hand-drawn carts left clouds in their wake.

Near the shore grass huts clustered closely. Now they saw houses of wood with picket fences around them and others of adobe with roofs of thatch. Straight ahead was a steeple. It rose above the nearly completed stone church where, the captain had been informed, he would find Dr. Judd, a medical missionary from the United States. He was an important man in the confidence of the King, then holding court on another island.

As they drew nearer they beheld an immense building constructed of coral blocks which could only have been cut at the shore and laboriously brought to the site on the backs of straining men or in crude handmade carts. Called the King's chapel, it would be known years hence as Kawaiahao Church, the Westminster Abbey of Hawaii. The roof was now being laid, and Dr. Judd was on the ridgepole working with the natives.

Dr. Judd descended and greeted the captain warmly. Were the men who accompanied him Japanese? he asked. Captain Whitfield replied that they had been picked up at some distance from the main islands of Japan, and that while he was reasonably sure, he could not vouch for their nationality. Not too far away were the people of the Ryukyu* Islands, said to be of mixed blood but under the control of Japan.

Dr. Judd well remembered the strange, almost starving, men who had been picked up on the shore of Waialua to the windward some nine years before. And only recently he had been made the custodian of another group rescued in mid-ocean by Captain Cathcart of the whale ship *James Loper*. Their disabled boat had been set on fire to prevent its becoming a menace to other shipping, after all movable property had been transferred to the *Loper*. After spending some time on the island of Maui and in Honolulu, during which they had been given food and shelter, the men had been sent on to Kamchatka. People in Honolulu had thought that the ocean-wise Russians might aid them, but no word of their fate had been received.

Dr. Judd suddenly remembered certain relics left by these men and dispatched a young Hawaiian for a neatly tied and labeled package. It contained twenty metal coins, a pipe and tobacco pouch.

With no money bearing the stamp of their kingdom, Hawaiians had been much interested in these strange perforated coins, so different from the Spanish *real* introduced by whalers. The money had been placed on exhibit at the Chiefs' Children's School, presided over by Mr. and Mrs. Amos S. Cooke of the American Mission. (One small boy is supposed to have tried to taste as well as feel the coins. Dr.

---

* Variously spelled Ryukyu, Liu-Kiu, Loo-Choo, LuChu, Lewchoo, etc.

Judd's journal entry under date of July 22, 1840, had been: "Last evening at Mrs. Cooke's Asa [G.] Thurston swallowed two coins and discharged next day.")

To Manjiro and his friends these exhibits were a joyful sight. The enthusiasm with which they fingered them seemed conclusive. But Dr. Judd was thorough. He produced a map of the Pacific and tried to find out from which point the men had come. They could tell him nothing, since the Japanese had never seen a map, and were obviously confused.

Finally Dr. Judd placed his palms together and bowed very low. Then he asked if this was the way they worshiped their gods.

The pantomime succeeded. Nodding, the men cried, *"Dai Nippon,"* and all five prostrated themselves. Surely they were Japanese.

With hospitality equaling that of the native Hawaiians, who welcomed all strangers, Dr. Judd took the captain and his charges to his home, "fifth house east of the government office belonging to the royal family," as Manjiro later remembered it.

Here they met the doctor's wife and daughter, Kinau. For months they spoke to Mrs. Judd as *wahine,* which means simply woman though they supposed it to be her honorable name.

The first day ashore was one of required routine. All newcomers must be registered by Mataio Kekuanaoa, the governor. For this purpose the Japanese were taken to the fort on the shore, which had been built years before as protection against Russian aggression. The walls bristled with cannon, but once inside, they saw nothing frightening. Kekuanaoa was an imposing man, the largest they had ever seen. Although his veins did not carry royal blood, he was the husband of a daughter of Kamehameha the Great, the father of two future kings and a royal princess. Acting as

royal treasurer, he had accompanied the second King Kamehameha to England, and had become world-minded. His
look and every movement carried the weight of authority.
Actually he exercised the dual functions of judge and governor, now balancing the scales of justice, and now wielding
the sword to execute the penalty he had himself imposed.

Yet he received the strangers with kindly interest. Told
that they had come from a far country and were destitute as
a result of shipwreck, he smiled reassuringly. "Aloha," he
said, and again, "Aloha." Whatever its meaning, the word
had a friendly sound.

When the required record had been made, the captain
left his charges, first putting silver coins in their hands and
promising to see them from time to time. Manjiro understood his benefactor's personal interest quite plainly now,
and had no fear that they were being forsaken. But henceforth they must take their orders from the governor.

He directed them to a small grass house with matted
floors near his own within the fort. The Hawaiian occupants vacated cheerfully and soon returned with a huge
gourdlike bowl filled with a grayish substance which they
began to eat with their fingers. There was enough for all,
and the strangers were urged to eat their fill. Brackish water
from a well at some distance tasted sweet after their long
privation.

At liberty to walk about the village, Manjiro and his
friends went often to call on Dr. Judd at the stone temple.
Some of the interior was of wood, hand-hewn in near-by
forests; part came from a country called California, they
were told.

A "castle"* near at hand was constructed of the same
coral stone as the frame of the temple and had a magnificent

---

* Thought to have belonged to Kekauluohi, the premier.

upper story "with room below for several hundred men,"
Manjiro noted.

Near the church were houses in which lived several families who were friends of Dr. Judd and Captain Whitfield.
They had strange customs, sleeping in curtained cupboards,
eating with a queer kind of chopsticks such as the sailors
used on the ship, and drinking the same dark brown fluid
made from parched beans like soya. The walls of their
rooms were painted in different colors, a sight the Japanese
thought worthy of note.

They observed that every seventh day these people went
to a grass-covered building in the rear of the temple to
worship a God said to have made the world in seven days.
This was like the New Year in Japan, the newcomers
thought, since the food was always prepared the day before
and all the shops were closed.

On their way to and from the fort the Japanese crossed
the towpath trod by Hawaiians in bringing in the ships.
This path reached well into the settlement and was the
principal thoroughfare.*

Men with flowers around their heads or shoulders were
hard at work widening other paths into streets. Everyone
seemed to be responsible to the governor.

As they walked about the village the newcomers saw men
something like themselves who wore long braids protruding
from their hats, and were told they were Chinese. They
looked curiously at them but could not understand their
language.

The Hawaiians appeared to have more reddish skin.
Their bodies were big and the corners of their eyes drooped.
One day a Hawaiian made a jesting remark to Goemon. He,
and the Chinamen, he motioned, had eyes like *this* (pulling

---

* The present Richards Street.

up the outer corners of his eyes). It was very friendly, but the strangers, taught from birth that they were descended from the gods, that "all beneath Heaven was Japan," were abruptly learning many things.

They frequently met men carrying canes the wood of which had a sweet odor. The newcomers did not know that in China, some years earlier, the Sandwich Islands had been called "Fragrant Mountains," and that because of high prices paid for sandalwood the forests had been denuded at the order of the chiefs.

The strangers were intensely interested in everything they saw: guns on a mountain behind the village, a second settlement they called Makai, which had a fish market at the cross streets. In another direction was a huge temple with windows of colored glass, truly wonderful to behold. They learned that priests from a far country called France resided at this place. A gun fired at the fort told the time of day, and they learned to count the blasts.

Each evening after they had returned to their quarters the Japanese discussed the strange things they had seen. Drunken seamen riding pellmell along the roads, disorderly houses near the shore and prisoners brought into the fort at all hours of the night must have shown them that lawlessness was rampant, that during the whaling seasons the "blubber men" ruled the town. Yet the air of freedom was something they were always to remember. No one seemed to question or restrict the movements of people entering or going out of the village. Complete strangers, they themselves were never looked upon with suspicion. In Japan, they remembered, the whereabouts of every man was known through an elaborate system of registration. Whenever a man went beyond prescribed limits he had to have a reason. No escape was possible, since at a long succession of barriers he must give an account of himself. That impressive power, the Tokugawa government, was thus able to know where every man and woman had been during the previous twenty-four hours.

Unable to rationalize what had happened, the friends could only marvel at their changed circumstances. It was as though they had been wrenched from reality. Stranger than they could appreciate was the fact that they were having their first taste of personal freedom in a monarchy under a Polynesian king whose predecessors had been despots.

One day, as all five squatted on their heels in the shade of their grass house, Captain Whitfield approached. He had given himself time to develop fully a plan long considered. He would return to the Islands before finally setting out for home, but now was the time to make the decision.

After inquiring into their present condition and prospects, he addressed himself through Manjiro to Fudenojo. He liked the boy Manjiro, he said, and wanted to take him to Fairhaven; he would give him a good education, which would include learning a useful trade.

The captain explained that he was a widower, but that Manjiro would be cared for by his friends—they were like one big family in Fairhaven. One day, perhaps, when he had a home of his own, Manjiro would live there as his son.

In a rapid fire of Japanese Manjiro explained words he did not fully understand. Often, he remembered, the captain had sat moodily before a picture of a beautiful woman which hung over his desk. Once, pointing heavenward, he had wiped tears from his eyes. That meant she had gone, never to return. With his dearly loved father dead, Manjiro could sympathize.

Fudenojo knew not how to meet the captain's request. He thought at once of his responsibility to Manjiro's mother— his honor demanded that he should watch over this young boy during his enforced absence from home. On the other hand, the captain had saved their lives. If he wished it . . .

When, by common consent, they left the decision to Manjiro, he eagerly declared his wish to go. He had been taken
into the captain's confidence some time before, but had
hardly dared to hope that such a wonderful thing could
really happen to him. It did not mean, he said defensively,
that he would not see his mother again. Why, the captain
knew all about the big ocean and how to overcome obstacles.
He would help him, and his friends as well, if an opportunity to return home ever presented!

*This was the first time in his life that Manjiro had acted
without group support—the first time that individual desire
had prompted his free action. The old dependence on
mother, village rule and tradition was suddenly swept away.
But there was still a patron; the gruff sea captain combined
in one person authority and tenderness. Security had not
been lost.*

When Manjiro left the landing in the ship's boat the
next day he, alone of the Japanese, was dry-eyed. As he
neared the vessel, delighted cries from the crew gave him a
feeling of welcome.

5

The World Unfolds

THEY soon dubbed him John Mung. Manjiro was pleased
that in part he bore the name of the ship that had rescued
him. John, he reasoned, was the foreigner's name for a
common man. There were other Johns on the ship but John
Mung was distinctive; it was his very own.

Members of the crew who at the time of the rescue had
seemed terrifying, were very friendly to the young Japanese.
One, who prided himself on being the brother of a school-
master, taught him the alphabet. Twenty-six letters seemed
much simpler than the forty-eight characters he had laboriously committed to memory in Japan. But to write across
the page, from left to right, instead of from top to bottom
was very difficult. He was constantly forgetting, then apolo-
gizing, a flush of shame spreading over his face.

Surprisingly soon he could set down simple sentences
and understand their meaning. But the sailors' adage,
"There has to be iron in a man before there is iron in a
whale," defeated him. He took his problem to the captain,
who patiently explained. Finally Manjiro's troubled look
vanished—he understood! And he was proud of the iron
within himself!

Following the path of the trade winds the ship arrived
at the Kingsmill, or Gilbert Islands, called "Nude Islands"

by Manjiro. It was very hot and the inhabitants were too indolent to build any but the rudest shelters roofed over with green foliage. Parts of their bodies they covered with the same leaves.

Some of the natives paddled out to the ship and the crew had an opportunity to barter. For bows and arrows they exchanged discarded links of chain and other pieces of scrap iron.

Still on a westerly course, the *John Howland* reached the Marianas, islands belonging to Spain. They were sometimes called the Ladrones, or as the early Pacific explorers had named them, Thieves' Islands. The ship dropped anchor off Guam, a popular rendezvous for whalers. The captain introduced Manjiro to several men from New England ports who rowed to his ship for an exchange of news. Much of the conversation had no meaning to Manjiro, but their contemptuous references to Japan struck deep.

When in the vicinity of Taiwan (Formosa) the captain summoned Manjiro to his cabin. Pointing toward Japan, he said with a negative shake of his head that he was sorry to be this near and not return the boy to his home islands, but it would not be wise to make the attempt. He must be patient. One day, perhaps, he might go back, but not now. He might lose his head.

Through the captain's binoculars Manjiro gazed in the direction of the lonely little island from which he and his friends had been rescued. He thought sadly of his mother. If only his going had not been so unexpected! There had been no *sakazuki,* no parting cup!

The captain and his alert crew caught whales at points fifty to a hundred leagues from the Japanese islands. Then in August, sailing to the east, they again approached the island of Oahu. But the wind and waves were so violent that they could not enter the harbor of Honolulu. It was a severe trial to Manjiro to be so near his friends, yet unable to see them. Perhaps they thought the captain was not a man of his word! He had promised!

In November the ship put in at Eimeo in the Society Islands, ruled by the French. Here the crew took on an extra supply of provisions. They would soon be ready, the captain said, to begin the homeward course.

Manjiro is strangely silent concerning a traditional ceremony staged by seamen for those crossing the equator for the first time. Was the arrival of a bewhiskered Neptune over the side of the ship and his boisterous antics as master of ceremonies only incidental in an unfolding drama, every scene of which taxed credulity? Or had Captain Whitfield forewarned the crew that the boy must be spared the rough treatment customary in those times?

On a day of quiet sailing, after again provisioning at Guam, the captain unrolled a map showing two oceans. He pointed to North and South America, explained to Manjiro that while the earth appeared to be flat, it was really round. He told him stories of Marco Polo, a fourteenth-century adventurer, who had ruled over a province in China and on his return to his native Italy had told of another fabulous country which proved to be Japan. He told of Christopher Columbus, who, sailing west, had discovered the New World for Spain, thereby revolutionizing the prevailing conception of the earth; and how within thirty years of his discovery the whole east coast of America from Greenland to Cape Horn had been explored and the globe circumnavigated.

Manjiro's mind, long shackled, leaped ahead. He was excited by such daring deeds, and his admiration for barbarians increased by leaps and bounds. Wrapped in her isolation, Japan, his own country, had taken no part in world expansion. It was small, on a big map only a number of specks in the sea, the captain told him.

Not long afterward Manjiro remembered that he had

been promised a beautiful sight on the homeward voyage. "Wait," said the captain, "until we round Cape Horn." Now, sure enough, there it was—a deep blue sea with floating objects that looked like scintillating jewels in the sun!

Icebergs towered several hundred feet. Dark objects at their bases proved to be walruses and seals with their young. Storms, increasing in intensity as they beat their way around the cape, gave the ship an almost superhuman power. The chanties of the sailors, which reminded Manjiro of folk songs in Japan, seemed to bring them through in times of great peril. After the storms had subsided a comet added to the majesty of the heavens at night. What a wonderful world, and how vast!

Manjiro's growing ability to comprehend a new situation greatly pleased the captain. By the time the ship was well into the Atlantic, and long before he could make out the chalky cliffs of Gay Head at the tip of Martha's Vineyard, he had made up his mind—he would see that the boy had every opportunity.

6

Fairhaven

MAY 7, 1843. At long last, journey's end! After an absence of three years and seven months Captain Whitfield brought the *John Howland* into her home port. He was glad to have the cruise behind him; well pleased with his 2,761 barrels of sperm oil. He had sold part of the catch at ports along the homeward route, and at Honolulu a returning New Bedford captain had obliged him by taking on as much as space would allow.* The high-grade sperm oil would find a ready market for many-prismed lamps and the manufacture of drawing-room candles; the remainder would be used in street and lighthouse illumination. Quantities of bone would swell the total receipts. Years of uncertainty and grueling work were forgotten in the first happy hours of home-coming. Captain and crew alike were jubilant.

Manjiro had heard much about Fairhaven as a whaling port and as a place to live, and now he peered over the bulwarks at Buzzards Bay. He could see New Bedford opposite Fairhaven on the bank of the Acushnet River. Both towns used the same harbor—ships docked at vacant berths on either side of the river. His gaze took in the shipping, the rising hills in the background, then fixed on the draw-

---

* This was a full ten years before the transshipment of oil from Honolulu became common practice.

bridge through which the ship was soon to pass. It was a marvel he would never forget.

Crowds had gathered to meet the ship, which had been sighted hours before by watchers on widows' walks atop houses. But the captain was intent on personal problems. One of his first tasks was to find a home for Manjiro. Finally, leaving a watchman on the deserted ship, he took his charge over the now closed bridge toward Fairhaven. They stopped many times for friendly greetings but came at last to the Oxford Street home of the captain's old friend, Eben Akin, a member of whose family was third mate on the *John Howland*. The captain believed that here his plan for Manjiro would find sympathetic interest.

After introducing him as "my boy, John," and recounting the story of his rescue, the captain requested the favor of temporary quarters. He himself must go to New York within a few days to report to his brother, who was his financial agent. When he returned he hoped to make permanent provision for the boy.

During the following weeks Manjiro was put to a severe test. Without the captain or his lifelong friends, he was at a loss how to pass the time. But it was spring; the contrasting shades of green in the countryside surely rested his ocean-weary eyes. Horse chestnuts with tapering, upright blossoms grouped like candelabra could scarcely have escaped his sense of beauty. Only to be imagined was the autumnal glory of the long rows of maples bordering the paths and village streets, for trees like these grew everywhere in Japan, in November so brilliant as to make whole hillsides a vast conflagration. Altogether, his new home was a place "sweet to see."* Gradually he began to learn the history of this section of the country, and to associate place names with the

---

* Herman Melville was referring to New Bedford when he wrote: "The town itself to live in is the dearest place in New England."

Sconticut Indians to whom the area had first belonged.

Fairhaven territory had been settled by Plymouth colonists, and the town claimed the distinction of having fought the first naval engagement of the Revolutionary War. This could have had little or no meaning to the bewildered Japanese boy, but Fort Phoenix, which had been erected to guard the harbor from the British, still contained its historic guns. Manjiro remembered these guns long afterward, even to their number and measurements.

Another landmark was an abandoned seventeenth-century farmhouse constructed of oak planks secured to the frame by wooden pegs in much the same manner as the planking of a ship.

The story of Manjiro's rescue had gone around the wharves, and curiosity was at a high pitch. A Japanese, was he? Well, if he was as obstinate as his countrymen were said to be, he wasn't worth a tinker's damn! When Manjiro passed unfriendly whalemen on the roads and heard such remarks, his longing for home must almost have overcome him.

Often he would steal away alone to the attic room in which his sea chest was temporarily stored, unfold the tattered kimono his mother had made for him and weep silently.

Was his mother being punished for his departure in accordance with Japan's cruel laws? He did not put the thought into words, but it chilled him. Only gradually was he pushing such horrors aside and building a world in which they did not exist.

He was unable to explain the intricacies of his code of honor. It seemed impossible for anyone in this new world to understand what to him and to all Japanese were basic obligations: *chu,* deference to the ruler, and *ko,* loyalty to one's parents. Only Captain Whitfield seemed to sense that filial loyalty was at the root of the boy's distress. It must

have meant much to Manjiro to be assured by this understanding friend that someday a way would be found for him
to return home and meet these obligations. But plainly
that day was in the distant future.

When Captain Whitfield returned from New York, he
brought a bride. Her name was Albertina, but Manjiro
almost instinctively added the title *Sama* (honorable). To
the young man she seemed of noble birth and very lovely.
She had heard much about him and had made up her
mind to receive him as a son.

Taking Manjiro with them, Captain and Mrs. Whitfield
drove to Sconticut Neck, a point of land jutting into the sea
four miles distant from the center of the town. Here they
proposed to develop a piece of good farming land. The captain was following a tradition which marked early settlers
of Fairhaven as good "farmer-sailors," with one foot on
land and one on sea. Manjiro was entranced with the pros-
pect of becoming a farmer, for in his own country those
who produced the harvests were but one step below samurai, or two-sworded guardians of the daimyo—feudal lords—
and their estates. At least he could pretend he was a real
farmer!

Soon after the two-story house was built, a hired man was
entrusted with the purchase of animals and farming imple-
ments. It was a time of great happiness for Manjiro. What
a thrill to ride a horse! For that he knew he could not do in
his own country. Only men of noble birth were permitted
such a luxury, having been trained from early youth in the
arts of riding and swordsmanship. Oxen provided common
transportation, but a farmer must dismount at the approach
of a gentleman, and a despised merchant meeting a samurai
must drop to his knees. The almost unbelievable freedom
in America was exhilarating!

But school was first in the captain's plan for Manjiro.
With the coming of fall he was enrolled in the Oxford

School on Farm Lane, taught by Miss Jane Allen, one of three sisters who lived next door to the Akins. During the following months Manjiro lived with the captain's Aunt Amelia at her home on Cherry Street. He was encouraged to use the familiar term "aunt," and the friendly atmosphere of her home soon put him completely at ease. Yet he was always eager to return to the farm for long holidays and week ends.

A sympathetic teacher, Miss Allen was quick to see that with proper guidance the foreign boy would become a good student. She encouraged him to remain after school hours and to talk freely, with the purpose of improving his English pronunciation. The letter *l* was the hardest of all. It was always getting mixed up with *r* and causing an embarrassed stutter. Only self-confidence could cure this, his teacher concluded wisely.

Since the relationship between them was very friendly, Manjiro was often invited to the Allen home for dinner. He became well acquainted with his teacher's older sister, Miss Charity, the cook and good angel of the household. It was she who kept the cookie jar filled, who watched his socks for holes, and he often sought her motherly advice.

So sped the happy days.

7

Prejudice

THOUGH critical of slaveholding in the South, New Englanders were not free of race prejudice despite a few struggling abolition societies. Portuguese from the Azores were beginning to settle in Fairhaven but by courtesy, or stratagem, had their own district. To many people a Negro was beneath notice.

Captain Whitfield, an ardent Free-Soiler, very soon took Manjiro to church with the intention of renting a family pew and enrolling him in the Sunday school. The reception was less than cordial, and he was not surprised to receive a visit from a church representative the following day.

In the family parlor, the deacon stood turning his hat in his hands and at length blurted out, "We have a section for Negroes and would like it if you would take your boy there."

The restraint Manjiro had long observed with wonder and admiration was now a saving grace. The captain rose, opened the door and bowed his caller out, his frosty silence a more stinging rebuke than any words.

The following week he took Manjiro to a church of another denomination, with similar results. A Unitarian church, which was just beginning to emerge from a storm of denominational criticism, received the boy without question, and the captain and his family at once became members.*

Captain Warren Delano I, a large shareholder in whaling and clipper ships and one of Captain Whitfield's friends, worshiped at this church. When the captain was away and Manjiro stayed in town, Captain Delano showed a friendly interest in the strange youth and occasionally took him into his own church pew. A descendant of Ephraim Delano, who had been a purchaser of one of the town's original "twenty acres," he set his own precedents.

The Delano home, a dignified, rambling house with stone walls enclosing formal gardens, was one of the most impressive in Fairhaven. A gleaming coat of arms over the door was evidence to Manjiro that the family was old and honorable. The rooms were richly furnished, with art objects from many parts of the world, chiefly China, to enhance their charm. The close association of the captain and his son with China, and their affection for the Chinese, had brought the Orient into the family circle of familiar things.

Captain Delano noted the polite manners of the Japanese boy and heard with interest the growing legend of his strict honesty. It seemed entirely possible that he was representative of the great mass of Japanese with whom trade appeared increasingly desirable.

In the neighborhood lived the Tripps, another pioneer family. Manjiro was not at first popular with other children because of his studious ways—and doubtless too because of the reflected attitude of prejudiced parents. But Job Tripp was drawn to him, and they often played *go,* a Japanese game somewhat resembling checkers; they also flew kites

---

* Only a short time later Ralph Waldo Emerson is reported to have canceled a lecture in New Bedford because Negroes were excluded from the audience.

which were the admiration of town boys. In later years Job, constant friend of his school days, was to say that Manjiro was the brightest member of his class, that he fairly "soaked up" learning: "Shy and quiet in his demeanor, always gentle and polite, and profoundly interested in his studies from A.B.C.'s to higher mathematics."

Almost as well as Fairhaven-born boys Manjiro now knew the names and rigs of vessels. Many times he rushed with excited throngs to see returning whalers pass through the drawbridge, eager for news of the catch. Almost everyone in town had a financial interest in the ships, whether as a large shareholder or as one who had invested "a score or two of well-saved dollars."

Often the inquiring youth climbed to sail lofts or watched figurehead workers. He knew only a little of the art, but he tried to tell them about wood carving in Japan. Sometimes he visited the ropewalks and saltworks or watched blacksmiths sweating at their forges.

The horizons of Fairhaven were as wide as the range of its whalers. Less and less an object of curiosity, Manjiro wandered along the wharves, stopping often to listen to seasoned crewmen telling their strange tales of insular people more curious than any he had yet seen and of fabulous Chinese mandarins. Always there was speculation concerning the people of Japan, shut behind a curtain of mystery. Again, for hours, he listened to heated debates on the subject of slavery. Unconsciously he was absorbing the democratic principle of individual rights and opportunity for all.

The Whitfields received good reports of Manjiro's progress in the Oxford School. Since the boy had a mind for mathematics, the captain decided to add the privilege of study at Bartlett's Academy, a large school on Spring Street near the bridge leading to New Bedford. Headmaster Bartlett was the town mentor; his school was "select." To his advanced courses in surveying and navigation he welcomed only the most serious students. He seemed pleased to enroll the captain's protégé when by extra study the boy had prepared himself.

In Bartlett's Academy boys and girls were taught in separate classes and discipline was strict. A boy who misbehaved was made to sit on a seat with a girl, a degradation not soon forgotten by taunting schoolmates. Apparently Manjiro was never a victim of such punishment.

Early in his course he heard of Nathaniel Bowditch, whose book, *The New American Practical Navigator,* was known as "the sailor's Bible." It had proved the value of celestial navigation and made dead reckoning a thing of the past. The author's death in 1838 had left a halo of romance about his name, and many stories were told of the self-educated Massachusetts man who in his twenties had been acclaimed the foremost mathematician in America. Manjiro was fascinated to learn that the great man's father had been a shipmaster and cooper; instead of following in his steps the son had attained a distinction of his own. This book would be the most precious possession in the world, Manjiro thought, and before long he had earned enough money to buy a copy of his own. Often he envisioned himself sharing this new knowledge with his countrymen.

About this time the whaleship *Sharon* returned to Fairhaven. It carried the news of its own danger and tragedy at sea and of the remarkable bravery of Benjamin Clough, the third mate. Here was a new hero, a nineteen-year-old boy whom everyone knew. Many whalemen, like Manjiro, had come in contact with natives of the Kingsmill Islands. To them the story seemed almost like a page from a book of personal experiences, though much grimmer than anything they had encountered.

Shorthanded, the ship had taken on several savage natives.

At sea again, while the boats were out in pursuit of whales, the natives had mutinied and killed the captain, who was alone with them. In spite of difficulty and danger, young Clough succeeded in getting aboard unobserved. Though singlehanded and badly wounded, he killed three natives and saved the ship. To men for whom danger was a matter of routine, courage had become commonplace, but the whole town applauded when the owners of the ship appointed young Clough a captain and announced that a new ship would be built for him. To the very young and stout-hearted, the story opened new vistas of opportunity.

By this time Manjiro was supplementing his studies with an apprenticeship to a cooper by the name of Hussey. The cooper and his family were "good but very poor living," reported Manjiro. "They gave us dry hard bread for supper and breakfast and dinner old Nantucket dumpling." This must have seemed poor fare indeed, for even at the farm—where frugality was the rule—there were always fresh vegetables and rich yellow milk. Finally, long hours and a starvation diet made Manjiro ill. Mrs. Whitfield interceded vigorously in his behalf. At the Sconticut Neck farm he was put to bed and nursed back to health. He then insisted on returning to finish his apprenticeship, for he had almost reached his goal.

Manjiro's foster parents were pleased and proud when he successfully completed his course at Bartlett's Academy. Since Captain Whitfield was soon to leave for another cruise, he arranged with his aunt to live with his wife, and placed Manjiro in charge of the farm.

Soon after the captain's departure his first son was born. Manjiro's delight knew no bounds when he was allowed to hold tiny William Henry. From that day until, directing the baby's first uncertain steps, he had taught the child to walk, he lost interest in the out-of-door activities which had formerly engrossed him.

Then came an unexpected opportunity. He was asked to make another whaling cruise. He had a hard time making a decision to leave the farm because he was proudly convinced that William Henry's development was his personal responsibility. The offer came from Captain Ira Davis, who had been a harpooner with Captain Whitfield on the *John Howland*. Now in command of the whaleship *Franklin,* which had recently been enlarged and converted into a barque, and in search of experienced whalemen, Captain Davis had suddenly remembered the Japanese boy who had been so eager for learning and who had studied navigation and knew the trade of cooper as well.

Manjiro was especially anxious to join the cruise because the captain told of recent experiences with Japanese adrift in the Pacific. He discussed the matter with Mrs. Whitfield, who from the beginning urged him to go. Her husband, she said, had written to the seamen's chaplain at Honolulu about him and he was half expecting to see him someday. Moreover, this was Manjiro's chance both to apply his recently acquired knowledge and to look up his friends of the shipwreck, who were presumably still in Honolulu.

Suddenly Manjiro was no longer a boy; he faced a future that would call for every ounce of his physical and moral strength. With a long backward glance at the turn of the road, he left the farm and sailed on the *Franklin*. It was early in 1846, long known as the "boom year" of whaling.

Leaving youth behind could not have been easy for him. Ahead he faced a challenge to manhood. Behind lay many happy memories. For instance, there was the May Day basket which he made and "hung" to a girl named Catherine Morten, who sometimes smiled shyly at him during recess. The custom of hanging baskets to one's friends in the springtime, accompanying each with an anonymous verse, particularly delighted him. It reminded him of poems fluttering in the cherry trees at home.

Hiding near by to witness the reception of his basket filled with buttercups, he had chuckled over the neatly penciled verse he had composed for it:

> Tis in the chilly night
> A basket you've got hung.
> Get up, strike a light!
> See me run
> But no take chase me.

Many years after, when Miss Morten was in her eighties, she copied the verse for Manjiro's grandson. She had never married and remembered Manjiro as a bashful admirer in their youth.

8

A Beckoning World

IN THE spring of 1846 the United States was at war with Mexico; by late May General Zachary Taylor, already victorious at Palo Alto and Resaca de la Palma, had driven the Mexicans across the Rio Grande.

As the *Franklin* approached Boston harbor, Manjiro doubtless heard many discussions on strategy. Fighting had been going on for some time, and reinforcements were rushing to the Gulf of Mexico, where a district called Texas was in dispute. From the deck of the whaler he observed what appeared to be many-storied forts along the shore. The whole aspect appeared to him strange and solemn.

After a stay of three days in Boston harbor, the ship sailed across the Atlantic, touching at the Azores and anchoring off Fayal Island. Then from the Cape Verde group it rounded the Cape of Good Hope at the southern extremity of Africa and proceeded east past New Amsterdam, an island which appeared to be uninhabited.

In this vicinity they sighted an object floating on the water. As they drew closer, they saw it was an immense turtle. They lowered a boat and went after it with harpoons, but succeeded only in wounding it. Manjiro could not resist such a challenge. With a knife in his teeth, he jumped overboard and swam to the struggling turtle. Riding astride it, he drove the knife into a fatal spot in its neck. Then he called for a rope and dragged his prey to the ship. The congratulatory shouts of "John Mung! John Mung!" constituted the first recognition of Manjiro's courage, and from that time on he felt a new respect on the part of the crew. For days, they all feasted on turtle soup.

Early the next year the *Franklin* put in at Kupang, on the island of Timor, one of the earliest American ships to touch at this Dutch port in the East Indies. Here a mixed population of fair Teutons, black-skinned natives with kinky hair, Portuguese, Chinese and Indians greatly interested Manjiro. Some of the houses reminded him of Japan, but he learned that the architecture was Chinese and that carpenters from China had built them. A medley of languages and strange customs contributed to a confused picture even after a month's stay.

In New Ireland, natives with faces and bodies smeared with clay seemed the most primitive people on earth. Having heard they were cannibals, the crew made no attempt to secure native shields and other coveted souvenirs. Solomon Island natives were said to be equally savage, and no attempt was made to land among them.

Finally, the *Franklin* sailed north and reached Guam, a port Manjiro well remembered. It provided welcome rest while repairs to the ship went forward. Discipline was relaxed and relays of crewmen were allowed to rest on shore.

During leisure hours Captain Davis took Manjiro on visits to other whaling ships in the harbor. The discussions concerning Japan's "pig-headed law makers" had a familiar sound, since Manjiro could remember hearing a wise man of his village years before refer to barbarians as "blue-eyed sons of pigs." Now the shoe was on the other foot.

He heard equally uncomplimentary remarks about the Ryukyu Islands, the chain of small islands, of which Okinawa is the largest, extending southwest from Kyushu—the most southerly of the main Japanese group—toward Formosa. Captain Harper, commanding the *Abraham Howland* out of New Bedford, had recently sent a boat in there and bitterly recalled the threats of the natives.

Such an attitude, all agreed, was a reflection of Japan's feeling toward foreigners since the Ryukyus were said to be under the control of Japan, and to a lesser degree of China, and paid tribute to both.

Turning to Manjiro, Captain Harper burst out: "That country of yours is a disgrace to the world! The government is not only damnably cruel, but stupid as well."

Manjiro was by now of the same opinion. The more he considered the matter, the more impressed he became with the need for a mid-ocean supply station for whaling ships. Why should not he himself open such a depot? The distance of the Ryukyus from Japan lent plausibility to the idea. Captain Harper's invitation to accompany him on a projected cruise nearer the Japanese mainland was declined since Captain Davis had plans of his own and did not want him to go.

A letter Manjiro wrote at this time remains to this day to testify to his deep affection for his benefactors in Fairhaven. Under date of March 12, 1847, he addressed Captain Whitfield, who was commanding the *William and Eliza* somewhere at sea. He enclosed a letter which he had received from Mrs. Whitfield and told of his newly formulated plan concerning the Ryukyus:

RESPECTED FRIEND:
    I take the pen to write you a few lines and let you know that I am well and hope you are the same. First thing I will tell you about the home the time I left; well Sir, your boy William is well all summer [until] the cold weather sets in. He [is] smart creature I never saw before. He will cry after me just quick as he would to his mother.

... Last summer we have got in about 50 bushels of apples, 115 bushels of potatoes and 8 or 9 tons of hay and have sold between 3 to 4 tons of hay, and we have plenty of milk to drink. I wish you had some of that milk.

Your wife is careful and industrious, respectful and good woman. I am glad you have a good wife. I hope you will never forget me, for I have thought about you day after day; you are my best friend on the earth, besides the great God. I do hope the Lord bless us whole.

O my friend I want to see that Boy more than little, he is cunning little thing I never saw before. When you get home give my best respect to whole. We were 10 months out 16th of this mo. After this we shall go N. and westward toward the Loochu Island Japan and I hope [to] get a chance to go ashore safely. I will try to open a port for purpose for the whaler to come there to recruit.

We came here to anchor 3rd of this month and saw a number of whalers. One of them touched the Loochu Island and send the boat ashore in order to see if they can get some refreshment. . . . One of the chief officers says to them in two days if you no sail he cut [lines?]. Name of this ship Abram Howland of New Bedford, Captain Harper. He is going to Japan Sea, he want me to go with him but Capt. Davis he would not let me go. . . . Here I have got letter for you written by your wife. She will tell you more about the home.

JOHN MUNG

By mid-April, the *Franklin* was again on its tortuous way in search of new whaling grounds, and a month later dropped anchor in the Bonin or Ogasawara Islands. These islands lying between the Marianas and Japan were of volcanic origin, and their fantastic shapes were a source of wonder to the crew. Castles, towers and heroic figures of men and animals seemed to pass in review as the ship approached Port Lloyd on the principal island of Peel, known to the Japanese as Chichi Jima. Skillful navigation was needed, but the inner bay provided safe and pleasant conditions.

Bonin, "Empty of Man," proved a misnomer. Here a group of white men and Hawaiians led an idyllic life. The colony had set out from Honolulu some seventeen years before. Its only responsible head was Nathaniel Savory, a Massachusetts trader. Because of his steadier character, Savory had risen in the esteem of his fellow colonizers above Matteo Mazarro, a Genoese who had been appointed governor by the territorially ambitious British consul in Honolulu. Mazarro had been given instructions to display the British flag whenever a ship appeared offshore. But he soon learned to make rum and consumed the fiery liquid so liberally that he was usually incapable of business.

Whalers found it a relief to deal with Savory. He was a loyal American who dreamed that the Bonins would become an important supply station under the Stars and Stripes. With seeds brought from Honolulu Savory had developed vegetable gardens that were the talk of the Pacific; his onions and garlic found a ready market as far as the southern island of Guam. At "Kanaka Village" taro and sugar cane were growing luxuriantly. Green turtles penned near shore were also stock in trade with the whalers.

While Manjiro helped fill water casks and transport fresh supplies, he learned of a Japanese, the sole survivor of a shipwrecked crew, who had been brought to the settlement by a Spanish ship. The man had later made his escape in a small boat of his own construction and had not been heard of since.

Though the knowledge was of no particular use at the time, Manjiro made note of the loose government of these islands and the excellent harbor in which the *Franklin* rode at anchor.

To his delight the ship sailed west and dropped anchor off one of the smaller islands of the Ryukyu group. Accompanied by Manjiro and five other members of the crew, Captain Davis rowed ashore. A native whom they took to be an official greeted them, and the captain turned to Manjiro for translation. To the disappointment of both, he could make nothing of what was said.

Soon another man of seeming authority appeared with a farmer driving two cows. By signs they offered the animals to the captain, and he in turn presented four bolts of cotton cloth. Further intercourse was obviously unwelcome to the islanders, and after the cows had been transported, the ship got under way. No great progress toward a friendly international relationship had been made, but Captain Davis felt that he had fared better than his predecessors.

Closer to Japan, they sighted little Torijima, where the crew lowered boats to fish. Memories of his earlier desperate plight brought thoughts of home to Manjiro. *Had his mother given him up for dead? Would he ever see her beloved face again?* His longing was intensified when in August the ship cruised along Honshu, the main Japanese island.

One day twenty or thirty fishing boats were sighted. Manjiro could not restrain his curiosity to know whence they came and whether the fishermen could point out the direction of his home province of Tosa. Captain Davis, understanding his interest, ordered the sails furled. Manjiro donned his Japanese kimono, tied a towel around his head Japanese fashion, and then beckoned to the occupants of the nearest boat.

They approached cautiously; when their courage appeared to fail, a ship's boat was lowered and Manjiro rowed alongside.

First he presented them with a pail of ship's biscuits, and then inquired the name of their native place. "Sendai,

Mutsu Province," the Japanese readily replied, but shook their heads when he asked the direction of Tosa on the island of Shikoku. The more Manjiro talked, the more silent they became. They offered a portion of their fish, but Manjiro, declining, endeavored to explain that the crew of his ship had been successful in catching all they could use.

This experience brought forcibly home to Manjiro the fact that in his zeal to learn English he had forgotten much of his native language, and that his ears were no longer accustomed to sounds which had been familiar in his boyhood. That there might be a difference in dialects apparently did not occur to him.

Anticipating a brief rest in Honolulu, Captain Davis now sailed east.

9

Reunion at Honolulu

It was September 1848. As soon as he was granted shore leave at Honolulu, Manjiro sought the friends from whom he had parted six years before.

He found only Toraemon, who was working as a carpenter and boatbuilder. He hastily laid his tools aside and took Manjiro to a quiet spot near the old fort in which the shipwrecked men had once lived. Here they could talk to their hearts' content.

The men left behind had been well cared for, Toraemon reported. The governor had continued to give them lodging and an abundance of taro, which had gradually taken the place of the accustomed rice. They were expert fishermen and were delighted to find *aku* (bonito), with which they were already familiar. They had taught the natives the use of poles in fishing and had become known for their skill. They sold their fish in the native market, and once in a while they were called into the country to help harvest taro and transport it on their backs to the governor's quarters.

But they had grown tired of an irregular life and finally applied to Dr. Judd for work. Jusuke and Goemon had been taken into the Judd household, with such outside duties as drawing water and cutting firewood. And Fudenojo—who had simplified his name to Denzo*—had gone as a waiter to a school for young chiefs—presided over by Mr. and Mrs. Amos Starr Cooke of the American Mission—where he had proved a trustworthy helper. The royal children, encouraged by their teachers to learn all they could of the country which lay beyond the setting sun and refused to deal with other nations, trusted and liked the steady Japanese. They had earlier become acquainted with Captain Whitfield, who was a friend of the Cookes, and a visit to his ship had been a delight.

Toraemon paused and his face saddened. Their friend Jusuke, he said, had never fully recovered from the leg injury sustained at Torijima. When he developed dysentery, Dr. Judd—who was now a government officer whom they addressed by his Hawaiian name, Puuku Kauka—had arranged for him to go to Koolau, a district some distance from Honolulu, where he might have real medical care. In a reclining chair he had reached his destination in comfort. But the prescribed treatment had brought no relief, and Jusuke had died. The sorrowing brothers appreciated the great kindness of a priestlike person by the name of Parker (the Reverend Benjamin Parker of the American Protestant Mission). Mr. Parker had made arrangements for Jusuke's burial in a cemetery adjoining the church at Kaneohe. He had read from a thick book like the Buddhistic *Indo,* and had been a great comfort to them.

---

* Fudenojo is known to have changed his name to Denzo for easier pronunciation by the Americans, and perhaps later to Kuke (Hawaiian for Cooke), since change of name was common practice in Japan. If this conjecture is correct, he possibly added a second Hawaiian name, becoming Kuke Kainoa. Records in the Archives of Hawaii show that Kuke Kainoa became a citizen of the monarchy October 25, 1844; his certificate was signed by Governor Kekuanaoa. Had he remained until after annexation, he would automatically have become a full-fledged citizen of the United States, the first Japanese to be so qualified.

Denzo and Goemon were reluctant to leave Koolau and the resting place of their beloved brother. A little later, when Governor Kekuanaoa and the premier arrived at that part of the island on an inspection tour, the missionary mentioned them. The governor remembered the brothers, and when he learned that they had no occupation, he granted them permission to develop a section of unused land. On it Denzo built a primitive hut and planted taro, sweet potatoes, millet and melons. A head tax of half a dollar annually seems to have been waived by the governor.

Goemon, assisting Mr. Parker at his church, was a regular attendant there. One Sunday morning, to his great amazement, he had discovered Captain Whitfield in the congregation, and after the service took him for a reunion with his elder brother. Now they learned that Mr. Parker and Captain Whitfield were old friends, having been neighbors in Massachusetts during their youth. The captain had made the trip around the island to Kaneohe to see both Mr. Parker and his Japanese friends.

Now Toraemon grew excited as he talked. The kind captain had suddenly found a way to ship Denzo and Goemon with an acquaintance, China bound, who had promised to do all he could toward landing them on Japanese soil. The captain, Mr. Parker and Dr. Judd had given them gifts and clothing. Denzo had presented what could be used from his little farm to his friend Parker and other neighbors, and had carried chickens and a slaughtered pig to Captain Whitfield.

News of the departure of his friends upset Manjiro's partly formulated plans, though he expressed pleasure at the captain's continued interest in them. Then one evening, as he was returning to his ship for the night, he was told that the two Japanese had just arrived in the harbor on the *Florida,* the ship on which they had sailed. He hired a canoe, skimmed swiftly out to the ship and was soon face to face with Denzo and Goemon. Unable to restrain their emotions at the sight of Manjiro, the brothers sobbingly told of their abortive attempt to reach the homeland.

They stated that, true to his promise, the captain had attemped to land them on what appeared to be a favorable section of Japanese shore. They were off the island of Hachijo, and near enough to see men working carabao in fields of rice. But the wind and waves were so strong that they could not beach their boat and had returned to the ship. They cruised along the coast for a while, awaiting favorable weather. Finally, with reckless disregard of rockets fired along the shore, presumably as a warning to the ship, they landed with the captain on the coast of Yezo, better known as Hokkaido, and made their way to a primitive hut. There charcoal ashes and half-emptied cooking utensils gave evidence that the inhabitants had fled in terror. They found Japanese garments hanging on the wall. Denzo called out in Japanese, and they waited for several hours, but to no purpose. The brothers implored the captain to leave them, but he refused. He had promised Captain Whitfield to take care of them and he had prepared a receipt which he wished to have signed by some Japanese official. There was nothing to do but go back to the ship.

On the return voyage they headed north for whales and spent long weeks near the Aleutian Islands and in the Bering Sea. Fog obscured the sun for days, becoming so thick that they were in constant danger of foundering on hidden rocks or ramming another ship. During one storm they were so buffeted about that for three days no food could be prepared and it was bitterly cold. The Japanese had been set to the task of striking gunwales with heavy sticks as a warning to other ships, and when they lagged they were dealt with severely. They had been gone from Honolulu for eleven months, and the experience embittered them.

On landing they sought Dr. Judd to explain their unexpected return and waited for an opportunity to visit their benefactor in Kaneohe.

As the disappointed men became calmer, Manjiro tried to console them by outlining his tentative plan to approach Japan through the Ryukyus. Yet he himself was disheartened at this latest news reflecting Japan's uncompromising attitude toward anyone who approached from the distant sea.

As Manjiro wandered about Honolulu village, he saw many improvements, among them the new palace of Kamehameha III, which had been completed three years before. It had a familiar look and as he studied it he saw that it had a widow's walk much like many residences in Fairhaven. A palatial dwelling which compared favorably with the finest he had seen had been built by a sea captain who had sailed in his own ship for China to procure rich furnishings, only to be lost at sea. His Massachusetts-born wife had, reportedly, seldom left the premises, still hoping that through some miracle the captain was still alive and would return to find her in her accustomed place. Manjiro knew that such a tragedy was common in seaports of the world; he had heard similar stories in Fairhaven. He could not know that this home with its sad beginning was to become historic Washington Place, in which one day a deposed queen would live.

At this time Manjiro met a friend who was to be of great influence in his future life. This was the Reverend Samuel Chenery Damon, Seamen's Chaplain for the port of Honolulu, to whom Captain Whitfield had referred him. The chaplain's specialty was homesick men, and he was at once drawn to the forthright young Japanese who spoke English and knew by name many who made Honolulu a regular port of call. His rescue by Captain Whitfield interested the chaplain even more, since the captain attended services at the Bethel when in port and occasionally sent him bits of news for *The Friend,* a newspaper Damon had founded in 1843. In addition to local news, *The Friend* chronicled the arrival and departure of ships and commercial statistics, including the latest reported price of whale oil on the New Bedford market; it printed the yearly almanac and such bits of world news as came in by ship. It had a wide reading everywhere in the Pacific, and when ships "spoke" at sea it was frequently one of the first things asked for.

At the Seamen's Bethel near the shore a flag floated each Sunday morning as an invitation to visiting seamen and villagers to attend church. In the basement was a supply of tracts and Bibles in all languages—all except Japanese, the chaplain ruefully explained.

Manjiro felt welcome also in the reading room which had been transferred to the home on near-by Chaplain Lane. Here seamen thumbed through American news-papers of remote dates, or inspected an interesting cabinet of curiosities which contained sea shells from many Pacific islands, bows and arrows, masks and spears.

Altogether it was a friendly place, with paper and fresh quills provided, and recourse to the chaplain should his advice be needed. Mrs. Damon, later to become organizer and active member of the Strangers' Friend Society, was also most hospitable.

In a comfortable nook Manjiro sat down to report to Captain Whitfield:

> HONOLULU, OCTOBER 30, 1848
> KIND FRIEND:
> ... I went to see Mr. Damon's and Mr. Smith's*
> family. They all glad to see me and told me you
> are a good friend to them and wanted me to write

---

* The Rev. Lowell Smith was a member of the American Protestant Mission and pastor of Kaumakapili Church.

to you and give best respects to you and your wife. Mr. Damon gave me paper and semi-monthly journal which contained some of your writings.

O Captain how can I forget your kindness, when can I pay for your fatherly treatment? Thank God ten thousand times and never will forget your name. . . . I was sorry to hear that your ship being leaky and obliging you into port before the season. The God will direct you into the straightest and clearest path of the sea. . . . We are lying with 700 bbls. sperm oil and have to go another season on the line. . . . Give my best respects to all your friends and your kind neighbors and my affectionate regards to your wife, Aunt Amelia and Mr. Bonney family. Tell them what quarter of the world I am in. I can never forget kindness they have done to me. It is hard for me to join words together and therefore come to close.

JOHN MUNG

Three days later he wrote his motherly Fairhaven friend, Miss Charity Allen:

HONOLULU, NOV. 2, 1848

RESPECTED FRIEND—

I take pen with pleasure this day to inform you that I am in good health and spirits, and hope most sincerely that these few lines will find you and all your friends enjoying health and happiness. I have received your affectionate letter by my friend and now return to you my warmest thanks for your kind wishes, and hope you will always find that I pay a proper degree of respect to the advice you are so frequently kind enough to give me, that my conduct may evidence the truth of the assertion, for believe me I shall always feel truly gratified in having the good opinion of friends.

We are lying with 700 bbls. of sp-oil and have to go another season on the line. I had couple of

chances to getting home, but being wanted at the
Nautical Instrument, and Capt. being unwilling
to let me go I could not. . . .
    Capt. unites with me in love to you all.

                                    JOHN MUNG

What more natural, that in idle hours Manjiro should
confide in Chaplain Damon his daring plan to return to
Japan? Or that Damon, the alert newspaper editor, should
weigh his prospects in the light of existing facts? He knew
well the plight of American whalemen stranded on Japan's
hostile coasts and the need for a supply station in that
distant area. Whether true or not, it was rumored that
among Japan's natural resources were anthracite and bi-
tuminous coal. And trade was indeed a hopeful possibility.
Much as he feared the outcome of Manjiro's proposed adventure, he admired the young man's courageous spirit and
could not but wonder what his chances might be. He
offered no encouragement, but said he would be glad to
help him should Manjiro make up his mind to go. "Think
it over carefully" was his parting advice.

    Three forlorn Japanese saw Manjiro off as he sailed to
continue whaling. Though the youngest, he had now become the acknowledged leader of the shipwrecked group.
His understanding of navigation and familiarity with the
waters adjacent to Japan, together with his firm determination to return to the homeland, had revived an all but
extinguished hope. But, Manjiro cautioned, they must
await his call. He would return to Honolulu to complete
arrangements.

    After whaling for three months the *Franklin* again cast
anchor at Guam. Captain Davis had begun to act strangely
at Honolulu, and he now progressed rapidly from morose-
ness to insanity. At length he became violent, and the only
recourse was to bind him with chains.

Now what to do? The crew held an election to select a new captain, and to Manjiro's surprise he received the second largest number of votes. He had always felt inferior on account of his size, for the burly whalemen towered above him, and they often swore raucously and threateningly. They sometimes attacked one another, and the sight of drawn blood seemed only to goad them. Yet somehow, though they sometimes laughed at the young Japanese, they appeared to respect his gentle nature and self-control. He felt loss of face when they made fun of him, but always tried to conceal his feelings.

It was his skill in navigation that raised him in the general estimation, and before long this ability was to save the ship. In approaching Luzon, they encountered a monsoon of terrifying proportions. Manjiro worked unceasingly without thought of food or rest, and the crew acknowledged that without him the ship would not have weathered the storm.

The new captain, whose place as first mate Manjiro had taken, had decided to head at once for Manila to ask help from the American Consul. This proved a wise decision; the authorities there agreed to provide hospital care for the unfortunate Captain Davis and eventual transportation to the United States.

The city of Manila seemed very beautiful in its situation at the head of a semicircular bay. The river running through the center of the city reflected ornate cathedrals and gave them a charm seen nowhere else. As at Guam, the people spoke Spanish, though there was a mingling of races, including Chinese. The members of the crew exchanged dollars for pesos and shopped in the native bazaars. In one Manjiro bought a woven hat of exquisitely fine workmanship and found it a comfortable replacement for his sailor's cap.

Early in April 1849 the *Franklin* headed north, skirted

Formosa and the Ryukyu Islands, then spent some time in waters near Japan. Again turning south to Guam, the ship crossed the equator and reapproached New Ireland and New Guinea. On the island of Ceram, Manjiro bought a brilliant red and green parrot and began to teach it English words, chuckling over the surprise he had in store for his Fairhaven friends. At Timor, an island divided between the Dutch and Portuguese, several crates of chickens were added to the ship's store.

With the holds full they began the homeward journey through the Indian Ocean. The ship sailed past Mauritius and Madagascar, and then rounded the "Cape of Storms," or Good Hope; and it was soon opposite St. Helena, famous among seamen for Napoleon Bonaparte's grave with its red-coated sentinel. In July they sighted the coast of North America, and in the latter part of September they cast anchor at Fairhaven.

Manjiro had now circumnavigated the globe in a successful whaling cruise of three years and four months. His lay would be $350.

But his heart was heavy and he lingered aboard ship after passing through the familiar drawbridge and seeing the crew depart. At Guam he had heard from a New Bedford captain of the death of William Henry, the little boy who had known him before he knew his own father, who had clung to his fingers while learning to walk. Manjiro had grieved secretly. Now, he knew, he must greet Captain and Mrs. Whitfield and hear from them the story of the fatal illness. Suddenly he hated the parrot; gave it away to a stranger.

10

Grieving Friends

IN THEIR grief and loneliness Captain and Mrs. Whitfield had longed for Manjiro's return. Now as the three gathered in the long intimate twilight at Sconticut Neck words came haltingly. Only as the weeks progressed did the full story of the long cruise unfold. The captain had heard from the first men ashore the news of Manjiro's promotion to first mate, and his praise was generous. To Manjiro it was the hour of his greatest triumph, though mixed with sadness. He was the first Japanese ever to sail a ship by the use of Western scientific principles. It was an outstanding accomplishment, he was often told.

The fate of Denzo and Goemon was of concern to the captain. He expressed disappointment that their attempt to return to Japan, which had appeared so promising as they sailed from Honolulu, should end in failure. But, he told Manjiro, the captain had done the right thing in refusing to leave them without first making contact with government officials. It would have gone hard with the returning men, he felt sure, for their story of involuntary shipwreck and kind treatment from foreigners would have been scorned.

Captain Whitfield presented Manjiro with a handful of Japanese coins received from another shipwrecked man to whom he had lent assistance during his latest cruise. Such needs for help were growing more and more frequent. With his new rating as first mate, Manjiro now found himself welcomed in homes to which he had previously been a stranger. And in several he saw objects of Japanese art, forming the nucleus of future collections, which had been brought to Fairhaven in earlier years by shipmasters in the temporary employ of the Dutch East India Company. War between Holland and France had forced Dutch traders, the only foreigners allowed in Japan since the expulsion of the Spanish and Portuguese Catholics centuries before, to engage ships of American registry to carry on their now dwindling trade. In entering Nagasaki harbor these ships flew the Dutch flag, but on the high seas displayed the Stars and Stripes lest they be captured by English raiders.

Manjiro met men who could tell him much concerning the negotiations at Nagasaki. He learned that a restricted number of Hollanders were allowed to live at this one port, though they were confined to a small man-made island known as Deshima. This was the single window through which the Japanese viewed the Western world. The resident traders were virtual prisoners, subservient to an amazing degree, and complained often of their lot. Every ship reaching Nagasaki from the Netherlands—one or two each year at last accounts—was thoroughly searched before negotiations could begin. Suspicious not only of foreigners but of one another, the Japanese officials made all transactions extremely difficult and prolonged. Why the Dutch endured such treatment was a question often raised. It was invariably answered with a sly wink and a jingle of coins in a trouser's pocket.

Manjiro found Fairhaven greatly changed. In September 1849 the town was talking not so much of whales as of the gold which had been discovered in apparently unlimited quantities in California. Exaggerated stories made the rounds; in shop windows gilded stones of enormous size appealed to overwrought imaginations. Newspapers carried banner headlines, and advertisements set forth the advantage of buying prospectors' outfits at home where prices were within reason. Soon Fairhaven—and New Bedford as well—was sold out.

The craze was so great that laborers left their masters and herdsmen their cattle, merchants closed their shops and men sold their household goods to raise money for passage and tools. Manjiro saw all this happening.

The recent death of the fabulous John Jacob Astor added to the frenzy. He had been an immigrant but had left an estate worth $20,000,000. Gold! Its glitter was in every eye.

Manjiro wanted to join the stampede, and Captain Whitfield encouraged him to seize this young man's opportunity. Caravans of covered wagons were being organized for the overland route through an uncharted wilderness. But Manjiro's mind turned naturally to the sea. He had many chances to sail as a navigator, for vessels of every description, many of them unseaworthy, were pushing out via Cape Horn. Others selected as their first objective the fever-infested Isthmus of Dairen, which had to be crossed by pack animals or on foot.

After some deliberation, Manjiro signed on a lumber freighter which was to follow the Cape Horn route. Accompanying him was a young Fairhaven friend, "Terry."

Now a man of experience, Manjiro called, as a matter of course, on the American Consul at Valparaiso. Precious metals were mined here, he learned, and there were many agricultural products. The town, with houses close together, and streets filled with traders, also interested him. While fellow crewmen rioted ashore, he sought to learn all he could of the place and its people.

11

Land of Gold

By THE end of May 1850 the ship was off California. With
the practiced eye of a mariner Manjiro looked with delight
on the distant shore line and on the splendid approach to
the great landlocked harbor of San Francisco Bay, perfectly sheltered from the ocean and a very important port
for all kinds of vessels.

Some fifteen or twenty miles opposite the mouth of the
harbor, the ship passed clusters of rocks which appeared as
sentinels. As they waited for a favorable breeze and finally
passed through a narrow gate, they could observe the ruins
of a Spanish fort on an adjacent bluff. The Bay was surrounded by hills and dotted with islands which seemed to
float on its surface. One, glistening white from guano de-
posits and covered with birds, was dubbed Bird Island by
the crew. What memories that name conjured up to
Manjiro!

But there was no time for disturbing thoughts. The captain was peering past the barracks of an American regiment
toward a hill, beyond which lay the settlement. His port
orders came briskly.

The shanty-and-tent town of San Francisco was all that

Eastern newspapers had pictured, but it held no attraction for those bent on pushing into the Mother Lode country. The *California*, flagship of the new Pacific Mail Company, had entered the Golden Gate some time before, the first steamer to bring gold seekers from the Eastern seaboard. She was reported to have been abandoned within half an hour after the lines were cast, with some of the passengers on their way to the mines before nightfall.

After a short stay at a water-front hotel, Manjiro and his companion took passage on a river boat driven by steam, the first on which they had ever ridden. Manjiro noted every detail. He preferred ships with spreading sails which plowed their way to the ends of the earth. But how much more wonderful these new creations that defied both storms and the doldrums!

At New Bedford Manjiro had seen a palatial new steamer which plied between that port and the island of Nantucket. That gleaming ship, gliding proudly by, a long streamer of smoke in its wake, became for him a symbol of America, which would remain vividly in his memory until the fateful day when, on his knees, he would tell of it to his breathless countrymen. . . .

The Sacramento River was alive with craft of every description, from a whaleboat to an ancient barque, all crowded with newly arrived men intent on reaching the mines. There was no fraternalism. Each man was for himself.

The two friends left Sacramento in a hired wagon, later resorting to pack horses.* Over precipitous passes they proceeded on foot, with tools and camping equipment strapped on their backs. In five days they had reached a high mountain capped with snow from which flowed three rivers.

---

* The report that Manjiro rode on a railroad from Sacramento is erroneous, since there was no railroad there until 1856.

After making camp they discovered agencies for gold and silver which had been established by the United States Government. These appeared to be doing a thriving business exchanging currency for flakes and fine gold.

The new arrivals, both strong and eager for conquest, were immediately hired by an enterprising Dutchman, who confined his own activities to a gambling hall. The promised pay was $6.00 per day, but when none was forthcoming at the end of forty days, they decided to strike out on their own account.

Intense heat within the mines drove them to the riverbanks where they learned to sluice gravel for gold. A day's washings sometimes resulted in twenty-five dollars' worth of the precious metal; sometimes they returned almost empty-handed to the poor food and makeshift beds for which they paid an exorbitant price. Bands of outlaws were at work, and peaceful miners, their pokes full of gold, were frequently sandbagged and robbed. The two friends witnessed acts of cruelty and heard murderous threats over card games.

When his capital had grown to a total of $600 plus several nuggets—the largest of which he was reserving for his mother—Manjiro decided that the time had come for him to make his way to Honolulu, starting point for the long-contemplated return to Japan. Since his waiting friends had little money, he knew that he must finance as well as direct the expedition.

Manjiro's first impression of America had been of a tolerant, bustling land in which a man had opportunity to make of himself what he chose and was master of his own fate. The exhilaration this new concept of life had produced was still strong in him. Yet he needed help in his contemplated venture. Ahead in the Pacific was a man on whose friendship he knew he could rely.

He bade his companion good-by and returned down the same river, presumably the Sacramento, by which they had reached the overland route to the mines. He found San Francisco more than ever a ribald town, hell-bent on gain and pleasure. Confidence of early admission to the American union had stirred a spirit of holiday recklessness. Makeshift hotels were full to overflowing. Ill and weary men were bidding for sleeping space in tents or corrugated iron shacks. Some slept on the steps of newly built churches. Brothels and lotteries of every description did a thriving business, while horse racing and bullfights drew other crowds. Bears pitted against bulls seemed to Manjiro an extreme form of cruelty.

Then suddenly, with the arrival of the S.S. *Oregon*, a Pacific Mail ship direct from Panama, came the first news that on September 9 California had been admitted to the American Union as the thirty-first state. Pandemonium reigned in San Francisco.

Though ships were coming in, few were going out, and none bound for Honolulu. The homesick Japanese saw his plans blocked indefinitely. Finally fortune smiled on him. News had spread around the Pacific that California was paying rocketing prices for potatoes, and enterprising merchants in the Sandwich Islands were sending shiploads whenever opportunity offered.

The *Elisha*, which Manjiro referred to as an "air ship"—perhaps showing his preoccupation with the revolutionary steamers—had recently arrived in port from Honolulu. Twice the size of an ordinary whaler, this merchantman seemed palatial to Manjiro. While the cargo was being discharged he sought out the captain and engaged passage for the return voyage, gladly paying $25. It was the first time he had traveled any considerable distance as a paid passenger. His reference to "stone for ballast" appears to indicate that the great cattle ranches of California were already being crippled by the thirst for gold, and hides previously trans-shipped to New England via Honolulu for the great leather and shoe industries were becoming scarce.

Eighteen days after clearing the Golden Gate, the *Elisha* was in Honolulu.

12

Reminiscences and New Plans

THE CAPITAL of the Sandwich Islands had grown unbelievably since Manjiro's last visit. Better streets, modern buildings and consular offices were evidences of a new prosperity. During this year of 1850 Honolulu, officially declared a city, was spreading out toward Waikiki and up the valleys. Old residents declared they were in the midst of a boom, and pointed with pride to the announcement in *The Friend* that in the prosperity occasioned by the whaling industry the number of retail firms had risen to seventy-five.

Toraemon was not hard to find, for he had remained steadily at work in the same shop. He immediately sent a messenger for Denzo and Goemon, who were living at the outlying village of Honouliuli.

While he waited, Manjiro visited the Seamen's Bethel and was received with evident pleasure. Chaplain Damon had returned only a few months before from a trip to upper California by way of Oregon as a guest of the captain of the U.S. transport and steam propeller *Massachusetts,* and he was anxious to compare notes on recent developments in the gold country.

The two travelers found much to discuss, and around the supper table at the home on Chaplain Lane they relived their experiences in the pulsing new state. Five-year-old

Samuel, who reminded Manjiro of his little playmate in Fairhaven, listened wide-eyed until candle-lighting, when he was put to bed by his mother, and the talk continued without interruption. Little could Manjiro know that this small boy whose large brown eyes followed him as he moved about would one day serve as an emissary from the Hawaiian Queen, Liliuokalani, at the Diamond Jubilee of Queen Victoria in England, would become a distinguished political and financial figure at the overthrow of the Hawaiian monarchy and have conferred on him by the Emperor of Japan the Order of the Golden Treasure.

Damon recalled incidents from the time he had left Honolulu—when the shore was lined with great crowds gazing with astonishment at "the second steam vessel in working order that had visited the Islands"—to eighteen days in the interior of California during which he "did not sleep in a civilized bed but once." Into Manjiro's hands he put several issues of *The Friend* which contained pertinent articles. The gold fever had become epidemic.

The intrepid chaplain had ascended the San Joaquin River via Benecia to Stockton, "a city of tents." There from the deck of a vessel serving as a storeship and moored to growing trees on the bank, he had preached the first sermon ever heard in that region.

He had visited a dying seaman of Plymouth, Massachusetts, who had previously been in Hawaii, and he had put off a projected seventy-mile overland journey to Sutter's Fort so as to officiate at his funeral. At Oak Grove, lying between the famous fort and Sacramento, he had been invited to take part in a rousing Fourth of July program where "almost every state in the Union had its representatives."

From New Helvetia, the settlement founded by John A. Sutter, Damon had proceeded to the "Mills" at Coloma, the spot on which gold had first been discovered. With his usual

A Daguerreotype of Manjiro

Compass drawn by Manjiro to illustrate his translation of Bowditch.

*O*N the pages that follow is a quick picture record of Manjiro's journey into the modern world and back into the arrested past of the Forbidden Kingdom. Virtually all of the pictures were drawn either by Manjiro himself or by two artists who worked at his direction, often with the assistance of his rough sketches. Our familiar objects and scenes observed by the unaccustomed Oriental eye come out subtly transformed and with unexpected points of emphasis.

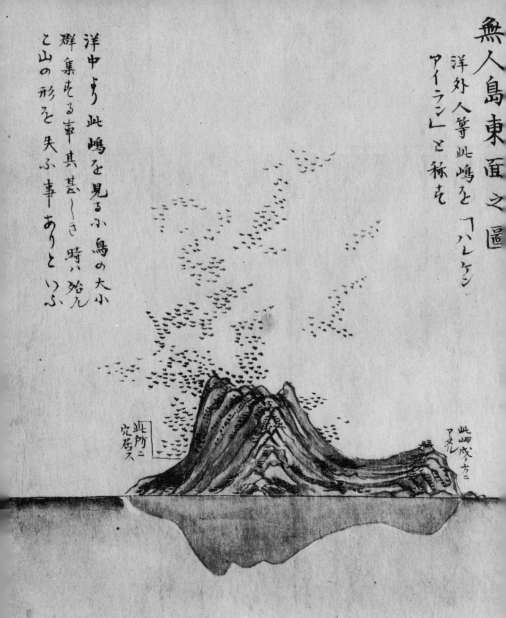

無人島東面之圖

洋外人等此嶋を「ハレケン
アイラン」と稱ゑ

洋中より此嶋を見る小島の大小
群集ゑる車其甚しき時ハ殆ん
と山の形を失ふ事ありといふ

此所ニ
穴居ス

此岬成ハ方ニ
アタル

HAILCAIN   I S L A N

The island on which Manjiro was cast away, called Torijima
by the Japanese but Hurricane Island by the Americans.
Manjiro gives it a phonetic spelling with a Japanese twist.

The castaways killing albatross on Torijima. This picture is from an anonymous booklet hand-blocked at Nagasaki in 1852.

アメリカの漁舩をまねく圖

Manjiro signaling the rescue ship, the JOHN HOWLAND

An American ship, per haps the JOHN HOWLAN itself. Manjiro invariabl put only one large star o the American flag.

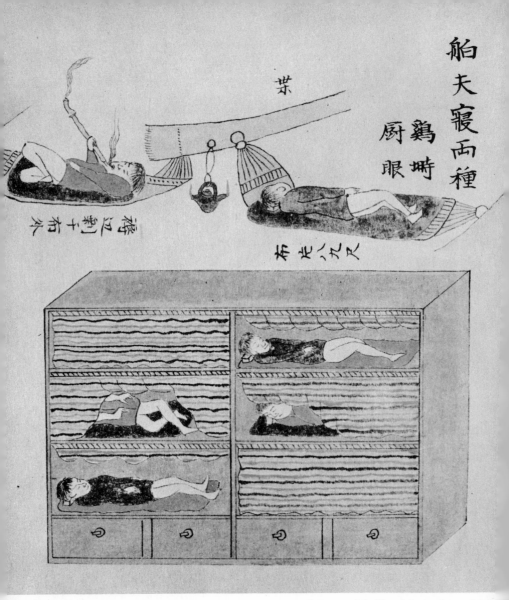

How sailors slept on an American ship. Manjiro indicated both hammocks and bunks.

Handling a captured who

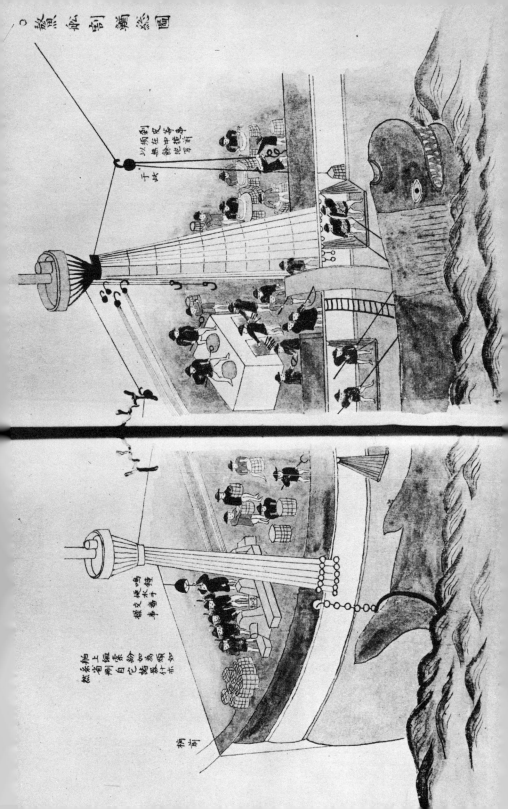

Honoruru (Honolulu) Harbor. The shrine at the harbor entrance is the artist's creation.

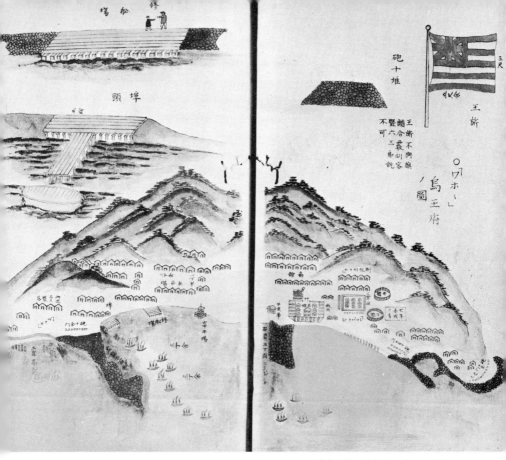

The Fort at Honolulu where the castaways were quartered.
The palace is near the shore just to the right of the center.
The flag of Hawaii is at the top.

ヌーバッホー港頭之圖

Fairhaven-New Bedford, Massachusetts, showing the drawbridge, drawn from Manjiro's sketch.

*Boston Harbor as Manjiro saw it. The rather elaborately
decorated sterns of these vessels may look unusual in
Boston but, as shown by the flag, they were American.*

Another view of Boston as Manjiro remembered it.

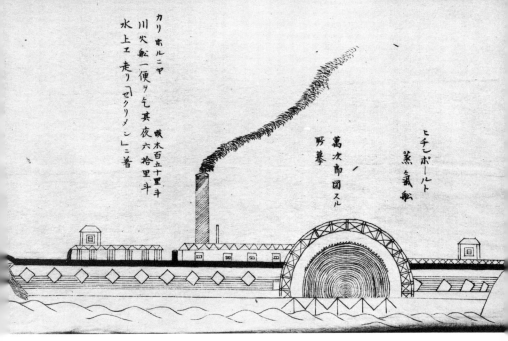

水上エ走リ「セクリメン」ニ著
川火転一便ヲ乞其夜六拾里斗
カリホルニヤ　　咸木百五十里斗

ヒチ子ボールト
蒸気船

萬次郎圀スル
野拳

Sidewheel steamboat on which Manjiro traveled from San Francisco to Sacramento. He was evidently impressed by the power of the wheel.

A railroad train as Manjiro saw it.

The KANRIN MARU, *which Manjiro navigated to San Francisco.*

Natives of Loochoo
(Okinawa)
as Manjiro saw them.

Courtesy of the Honolulu Academy of Arts

琉球圖圖

此地ノ形チ角ナキ龍ノ如シ
因テ流虬ト云トゾ國中ニ
三省アリ中山ハ中頭省
山南ハ島尻省山北ハ
國頭省之此屬所
三十六アリコレ
ヲフタ間ト云ヲ
間切各領
部間切縣切城
生切ヲ各領
按主主ト云ヘ

東

西

Courtesy of the Honolulu Academy of Arts

Manjiro's map
of Okinawa.

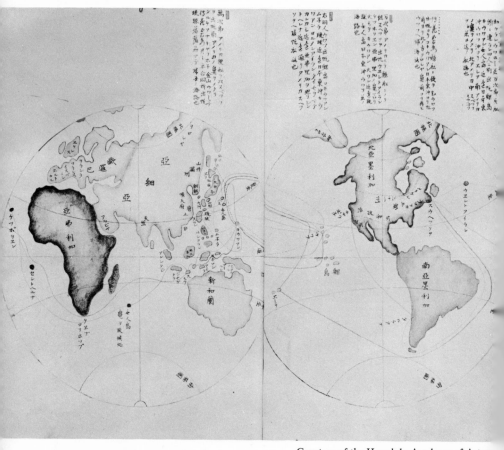

Hemisphere maps showing Manjiro's whaling cruises. For teaching purposes he marked his map entirely in Japanese characters.

concern for those in difficulties, he had visited an encampment of Sandwich Island gold diggers there. They were
eager for his advice in solving many problems, especially
on how they should deal with the mounting prejudice
against foreigners, an attitude they found difficult to understand. When he left the encampment, the Honolulu chaplain carried a packet of letters addressed to native friends.

When he returned to San Francisco, he found that the
population of the city had nearly doubled during the month
he had traveled about; Irish potatoes, valued at $2.00 a bar-
rel in Honolulu, were selling for $27.50 per barrel in San
Francisco. Now familiar with barter and world trade,
Manjiro doubtless found such stories astonishing.

The two travelers could compare notes on virgin forests
and other magnificent scenery, but the elder man had had
much the richer experience in meeting and talking with
people of many interests. Among others, he had met W. M.
Gwin of the United States Immigration Service, soon to be
elected senator by the new state.

With the foresight of a W. H. Seward, and three years
before that statesman addressed the United States Senate
on the decline of Europe and the future expansion of
American commerce in the Pacific, Damon wrote as his ship
sailed from San Francisco: "Over the waters of this bay . . .
a vast commerce is soon to pass. . . . Here is the wealth—here
tends the tide of immigration; that tide cannot be turned
aside. It will ere long reach the islands of the Pacific." So
impressed was he with Seward's later prophesy that he combined it with woodcuts of the Honolulu Bethel and Seamen's Home as a heading for *The Friend*. Strikingly like
his own were Seward's words: "The Pacific Ocean, its shores,
its islands and the vast region beyond, will become the chief
theatre in the world's great hereafter."

When Manjiro told Mr. Damon that his mind was made
up to return with his friends to Japan, the alert editor had

even more important news for him concerning developments in the mysterious country forbidden to the West.
Two years previously *The Friend* had carried the story of
the desertion of fifteen crewmen from the American whale
ship *Lagoda*. In rebellion against cruel treatment at the
hands of their captain, these men had made their escape in
the Japan Sea and landed on the northern island of
Hokkaido.

According to later reports, they had a stormy time. At first
they had been cast into prison near the Straits of Matsumae,
but had made their escape, only to be captured and confined
in an offshore boat. They had escaped a second time, and
been recaptured. Ordered to Nagasaki for trial, they had
been thrust into a common prison, said to be a former
Catholic church built two centuries before by Portuguese
or Spanish priests who had been persecuted and finally
driven from the country. The crewmen had been forced
to trample on a metal plate embossed with the crucifixion
scene as evidence that they were not Christians.

Dutch interpreters had asked if they had come to Japan
as spies, but the frightened men had declared their innocence and explained their proximity to the Japanese shore
with the statement that they had been in search of whales.
"Whales, do you eat them?" their examiners had queried.

Questions had seemed endless, and one man had become
so overwrought that he had taken his own life. After a
third jail break, the prisoners had been shut up in cages and
their feet made fast in stocks.

Finally Commander Glynn of the U.S.S. *Preble*, stationed in China, had rescued these Americans after being
informed of their plight by Dutch traders writing from
Batavia.

Mr. Damon took personal satisfaction that a story written
by him and published in *The Friend* had informed Com-

mander Glynn of the fact that still another American was believed to be in Japan, probably as a prisoner. This was Ranald MacDonald, son of the chief factor of the Hudson's Bay Company in Oregon. His mother was an Indian woman known to the pioneer white families as Princess Sunday. Earlier MacDonald had met some Japanese fishermen who had been borne on the Pacific current from Japanese waters to the American continent near Sitka, Alaska, and thence to Oregon. After some association with them he had made up his mind that they sprang from the same racial stock as he, a theory of interest to later ethnologists. Discontented with life at sea, and an adventurer at heart, MacDonald had planned to force his way into Japan, and to that end persuaded the captain of a whale ship sailing from Hawaiian waters to let him off in a ship's boat somewhere along the Japanese coast.

Nothing of MacDonald's progress had been known in Honolulu until the receipt of a letter from one of his shipmates, who wrote that the captain had fulfilled his agreement. They had last seen MacDonald as he waved good-by from his small boat. The boat was considered seaworthy and he had a stock of provisions, but his fate at the hands of the Japanese was a matter of grave concern.

One of Commander Glynn's officers had written Damon from Hong Kong: "Had it not been for this new knowledge we would not have known that MacDonald was in Japan before we sailed for that port, and from our observations of Japanese character we have good reason to believe that they themselves would never have mentioned the fact . . ."*

---

* MacDonald himself took a different view of Japanese character. He recorded in the *Narrative* published after his death: "They are naturally the cleverest people I know of. I say 'cleverest,' not in the sense of deceit, but in its highest and purest meaning. All they require is light from without."

MacDonald was rescued before this letter was written, and his experiences had become a matter of public record. He, also, had been compelled to trample on the Christian symbols, which were, he was told, the devils of Japan. But his treatment had been less severe than that of the *Lagoda* crewmen owing to the fact that several Japanese scholars had come to him seeking tutelage in English and he had been a willing teacher. Though all the prisoners had been confined in the same city, they knew nothing of one another until delivered to Commander Glynn on board the *Preble*.

Editor Damon was jubilant. "This rescue," he commented, "opens a new chapter in the intercourse of foreigners with the exclusive Japanese."*

---

* Damon's part in keeping the public informed of important events in the Pacific arena had been remarkable. On February 2, 1846, his newspaper published—for the first time anywhere—an account of Captain Macator Cooper's unsuccessful visit to Japan on the whale ship *Manhattan*.

This was followed on September 15 of that year by a report of the abortive attempt of Commodore James Biddle on the U. S. *Columbus* to enter Japan for the purpose of opening friendly intercourse. The full story had been written while the *Columbus*—the largest ship seen at Honolulu up to that time—was lying in the outer roads on the return voyage to the United States.

On December 1, 1848, Damon published an account of the departure of Ranald MacDonald from Lahaina, Maui, the previous year. Extracts from the letter of one of MacDonald's shipmates, written at sea June 28, 1848, had brought the recorded adventure to the point of MacDonald's leaving the ship off the coast of Japan.

The alert Damon had also placed himself heavily in the debt of Pacific whalemen when in November 1848 he gave publicity to the discovery of rich whaling grounds in the Arctic. By the following October fifty vessels had been induced to steer for Bering Strait and Icy Sea, with spectacular results. The Arctic region then rivaled waters off Japan as a productive whaling ground, and had greatly increased business in the Sandwich Islands, since during the frozen winter ships sought Honolulu or Lahaina for rest and the purchase of supplies.

The subsequent discovery of the Black Current, called Kuro Shiwo by the Japanese, was announced in *The Friend*, giving American navigators and oceanographers their first knowledge of that mid-ocean phenomenon. This was the two-mile-an-hour current into which Manjiro and his companions had drifted and which had swept them to the uninhabited island from which they had been rescued by Captain Whitfield.

13

Outfitting the Adventurer

DENZO and Goemon entered at once into Manjiro's plan to attempt a return to Japan. Goemon had married a Hawaiian girl, however, and she was not easy to persuade. Filial loyalty meant little to a Polynesian.

Toraemon flatly refused to leave Honolulu. He had worked steadily as a carpenter and was happy in his new life. Besides, he argued, Denzo and Goemon had failed in one attempt to reach their homes. He saw no hope in another attempt. After lengthy argument Manjiro and the brothers concluded it was futile to try to change Toraemon's mind.

Manjiro deposited his earnings with the chaplain and drew on them as needed for the purchase of a whaleboat and supplies. He then made an effort to locate a sympathetic sea captain bound for China who would carry him, his friends and the whaleboat to the vicinity of the largest of the Ryukyu Islands. They would work to pay their passage.

He did not have long to wait. The *Sarah Boyd,* a merchantman bound from Mazatlan to Shanghai, arrived in the harbor in early November. Manjiro learned that the master was Captain Whitmore of Alabama. He had heard the name and the chaplain knew of him indirectly.

Though skeptical of reaching Japan in this or any other way, Captain Whitmore was interested in the proposed venture. However, he said quite frankly that it would be a hardship to lose three members of his crew before the voyage was completed. Manjiro replied that his friends were unskilled, but he himself would work extra hard. If, when they reached the Ryukyus he had not earned their passage, he would go on to China provided the others might be allowed to go ashore. This arrangement was satisfactory to the captain and he signed on all three.

Manjiro was all the more grateful because of a disheartening experience shortly before with another sea captain bound for China. Manjiro had visited the ship and talked with five destitute Japanese aboard. They were from Kishu and had been shipwrecked off Shimoda after freighting oranges and lacquer goods to Yedo, the capital of the Shogun. To get their full story Manjiro had to seek out his friends as interpreters. This made him realize anew his deficiencies in Japanese.

The captain of that ship had promised to take Manjiro and his friends on to China with his five Japanese crewmen. To express his gratitude, Manjiro immediately set about mending oil casks, and the captain discovered he had an expert cooper. But a dispute arose when demands grew excessive. Great piles of broken casks and furniture were brought from the hold for Manjiro to repair. The young man grew angry. He had begun his work early to express good will; to be ordered about left him smarting. Finally he told Denzo that the captain was a slave driver, and he could not endure such treatment over a period of weeks or months. The three of them left the ship. For the first time Denzo realized that Manjiro had a quick temper.

The happy turn of affairs now raised their spirits. They added a mast to their newly acquired whaleboat and began stowing away supplies. They decided to call their boat the *Adventurer* and painted the name on the stern while many curious friends came and went.

Meanwhile, Chaplain Damon had not been idle. As a newspaper editor, he could draw public attention to the venture and secure help. He recounted the history of the shipwreck, outlined the present plan and made a direct appeal:

> ... To complete the outfit of these men is wanted a compass, a good fowling piece, a few articles of clothing, shoes, and a nautical almanac for 1850. The undersigned will be responsible for the safe delivery of the articles referred to.
>
> S. C. DAMON

The friendly chaplain made a personal call on the Honorable Elisha H. Allen, United States Consul at Honolulu, which resulted in the execution of a paper referred to by the editor as "a duly certified document of American citizenship, well supplied with seals." This, he thought, might have some weight with the Japanese authorities. Manjiro thus became the first Japanese to be furnished with an American passport. It stated the American desire for trade, a point often stressed by Damon in his talks with Manjiro and added at the editor's request. The full document reads:

> CONSULATE OF THE UNITED STATES
> HONOLULU, HAWAIIAN ISLANDS
>
> To whom these presents shall, doth or may come: I, Elisha H. Allen, Consul of the United States of America, for Honolulu, Hawaiian Islands, send greetings:
>
> Know ye, that satisfactory evidence has been produced to me that John Manjiro, Denzo and Goemon, left the southeast part of the island of Nippon, Japan, in a fishing vessel and were wrecked; and after remaining on an uninhabited island for about six months, they were taken off by Captain Whitfield of the American whaleship, *John Howland,* who brought them to the Sand-

wich Islands. Denzo and Goemon remained here; Manjiro went cruising for whales, and in the year eighteen hundred and forty-four [*sic*] reached the United States where he was educated. Last October he arrived here again, after visiting California, the gold region of the United States of America.

Captain Whitmore has kindly consented to take this company in the bark *Sarah Boyd,* a vessel belonging to the United States of America, and leave them near the Loo Choo Islands. Some friends here aided them in making preparations for their voyage and I trust they may be kindly treated by all persons whom they meet.

I am informed by the Chaplain of the Seamen's Friend Society that Manjiro has sustained a good character and has improved in knowledge. He will tell his countrymen of Japan how happy the Americans would be to make their acquaintance, and visit them with their ships, and give gold and silver for their goods.

Given under my hand and the seal of this consulate at Honolulu this thirteenth day of December, in the year of our Lord, eighteen hundred and fifty.

[Signed]

ELISHA H. ALLEN

U. S. Consul

With meticulous care, Manjiro stowed away necessary supplies and gifts for family and village friends. Needles and thread, scissors, buttons, soap, patent medicines, pots and pans, a looking glass, coffee and white sugar were items long planned for his mother. Of more general interest were fine tobacco, matches, panes of glass, paint and brushes, lead, chisels, axes, etc. An extra strop and razor and a dependable sea-going clock were among his personal luxuries. Carefully wrapped and protected against the weather were several precious books, including Bowditch's *New*

American Practical Navigator, a survey text, a *Life* of George Washington, an American atlas, and a nautical almanac. The instruments for navigation were placed ready for use, while canned food was stored against a day when they might be faced with starvation. Equally important were water casks filled on the day of departure.

Suddenly remorseful because of his failure to communicate with Captain Whitfield before leaving California, Manjiro now wrote him a letter expressing gratitude for his fatherly care and outlining his present plans. He was comforted by the thought that the captain would understand his urgent need to see his mother, because his absence from home violated the family code of honor:

> . . . I never forget your benevolence to bring me up from a small boy to manhood. I have done nothing for your kindness till now. Now I am going to return with Denzo and Goemon to native country. My wrong doing is not to be excused but I believe good will come out of this changing world, and that we will meet again. The gold and silver I left and also my clothing please use for useful purposes. My books and stationery please divide among my friends.
>
> JOHN MUNG

Last-minute gifts from Chaplain Damon were several marked copies of *The Friend* and a complete file for the year 1850. This material was to refresh Manjiro's memory concerning important international matters of which they had talked. The idea had been growing in the editor's mind that since the Japanese officials scorned American attempts at friendly intercourse, one of their countrymen might, by some twist of fate, be able to get the main idea across. It would be good fortune indeed if the material were to fall into the hands of Japanese officials.

The sailing of the *Sarah Boyd* with her unusual crew and cargo caused a stir in the village, and warmhearted Hawaiians expressed their aloha with garlands of flowers. Well aware of the dangers ahead, not only on the sea but in Japan itself, Damon tarried to the last, then added his final blessing.

In the next issue of his newspaper he shared his hopes with his readers:

> . . . We shall anxiously wait to learn the success of Captain Mung's expedition. He is a smart and intelligent young man, and has made good use of his opportunities, being able to speak and write the English language with tolerable accuracy. Should he succeed in reaching his native land in safety, his services should be of importance in opening an intercourse between his own and other countries. He would make an excellent interpreter between the Japanese and the English or Americans.
>
> Success to John Mung commanding the *Adventurer!*

A practical dreamer, was Editor Damon. He had entrusted to a bilingual interpreter the most comprehensive digest of American opinion yet prepared for the Japanese.

In these latter days of 1850 as Manjiro was heading for the land of his birth, Charles Dickens was publishing in England his famous *Household Words,* a series of imaginary journeys to little-known sections of the globe. His sources on Japan were Dutch, and because such facts were not readily obtainable, his stories were avidly read. "Japan," wrote Dickens, "is a country in which not a soul does as he pleases, and from which the commerce of the world is shut out. It is their policy not to permit their own nationals to

venture into foreign seas, and even if it should occur in a
sailing accident, life being cheap, no redress is provided
for."

And in Japan itself, Takano-Choei, a farsighted scholar,
lay dead after years of imprisonment and cruel persecution
for having written "The Story of a Dream," an imaginary
tale depicting a world of opportunity outside Japan and
advocating opening the ports to commerce.

14

Ashore on Okinawa

EARLY IN the year 1851 the *Sarah Boyd* rode a stiff gale toward the largest of the Ryukyu Islands.

By this time Captain Whitmore was so impressed with Manjiro's industry and knowledge of navigation that he felt he could not spare the young man. Manjiro, he knew, would stick to his bargain and continue on with the ship. But Denzo and Goemon refused to part from their leader. Reproachfully Denzo told the captain they too would go on to China.

Captain Whitmore could not deny his obligation to a man who had worked faithfully and well. But he wondered too about the wisdom of the plan. These islands were generally conceded to be a listening post for Japan. What would happen when the story of these wanderers reached the central government?

"Laws in force here will not allow you to land," he warned them. "If you try, you will be beheaded. You already know this. I recommend that you do not make the attempt, but finish the trip with me and return to the United States."

Manjiro replied, "I thank you, sir. I know the laws of Japan, but over there is my mother. If I do not carry out my plan, I will fail in my duty to her. So I will go, speaking only the truth and not fearing punishment."

Deeply moved, Captain Whitmore answered, "I realize how you feel and am willing to leave the decision to you. We will get along without you. I give you my blessing and hope that your plan will succeed."

They waited one night for the wind to abate, then brought the ship closer to the land. Chart in hand, the captain discussed with Manjiro the best place to land. "We will be watching you," he said, "and will not sail until we are convinced that you have not changed your mind."

Manjiro's last act on the ship was to present the captain with a gift taken from the *Adventurer's* store. He had previously entrusted to him a letter adressed to Toraemon, in whom, he greatly feared, the magnet of filial loyalty had lost its power. This message was to assure him of their safety thus far on the journey and to urge him to work his way home in a similar manner.

When his boat had been lowered, Manjiro hoisted the sail. Rain mixed with hail was falling and it was bitterly cold. Remembering their experience in northern seas, the brothers were greatly alarmed, Goemon crying aloud in distress. Manjiro encouraged them by saying that their situation was as nothing compared to meeting a whale in mid-ocean. Then he lowered the sail, took the oars from Goemon's trembling hands and rowed with all his strength. Late in the afternoon he silently observed the *Sarah Boyd* under full sail fast disappearing from sight. *No turning back now!*

Waiting for the first streaks of dawn, Manjiro and Denzo dozed from sheer exhaustion, while Goemon remained on watch. When he saw men carrying fishing poles on the shore, he woke the others, and the *Adventurer* was brought to a point from which Denzo could swim to the land. He was the most fluent in Japanese, and they thought that his greater age would command respect.

With one exception, the fishermen fled at his approach. When Denzo bowed and politely asked the remaining man the name of the island, there was no response. Disappointed and chagrined, Denzo returned to the *Adventurer*. This seemed to be another place where they could not be understood and where people ran away at the approach of strangers. He was recalling his bitter experience three years before, and expressed the fear that the same stalemate awaited them here.

But, Manjiro reasoned, if there were people there must be a settlement where there would surely be someone who could understand Japanese. He made the *Adventurer* fast to a projecting rock and, carrying a loaded pistol, landed with Denzo. He felt that they must be prepared for any emergency.

After a short distance they met a group of islanders and Denzo again inquired the name of the place. "This is Mabunimagiri, Ryukyu Island," replied a voice in Japanese. "Where did you come from and what is your purpose in coming here?"

Cheered by the sound of their mother tongue, the wanderers told their story; whereupon the young native assured them that since they were Japanese they would not be mistreated. He pointed to a sheltered cove and under his direction Goemon brought the *Adventurer* to shore.

Seeking fresh water, Manjiro took an empty bottle from the boat. This was filled by an obliging onlooker, while others hastened to bring sweet potatoes and sugar corn. A fire was soon built and coffee boiled. Bread and cake, brought from the ship, completed the first meal of Manjiro and his friends on shore. They were surrounded by curious natives who gravely studied their faces, then in twos and threes examined the strange clothing, fingered buttons, explored pockets. The unshaven heads of the newcomers were objects of prolonged discussion. Occasionally there was muffled laughter.

But soon the air was electrified by the arrival of Satsuma officials on horseback. They demanded to be shown the boat in which the strangers had come. Their form of address was not that of the common people, yet they were easily understood. Every word was a command. "Hand over your boat and cargo," followed the seizure of Manjiro's pistol.

The strangers were next given to understand that they must report at another place they later understood to be Naha, the capital and chief seaport. Three guards accompanied them. The road over which they traveled was muddy from heavy rains and in the deep ruts they often stumbled. As darkness fell rush torches were lighted.

They had traveled continuously from four o'clock in the afternoon until near midnight. As they neared the capital, a messenger brought orders for them to retrace their steps. This strange maneuver was apparently to forestall a meeting between them and Dr. B. J. Bettleheim, the only foreigner in the Ryukyus. He was an Austrian, a convert from Judaism, who, with his English wife, had been sent to the islands by a London Missionary Society. The missionary had been constantly spied on and his one convert was stoned to death. He and his wife were frequently hooted in the streets, though they were often called on for medicines when native potions failed. They might have been treated even worse if the local authorities had not been afraid of British gunboats.* Manjiro and his friends were never allowed to meet these unwelcome foreigners.

Apparently realizing that without additional food the

---

* Dr. Bettleheim and his family were later moved to China by Commodore Perry.

men under their escort could not proceed, the guards shared
bowls of rice with them. Their dexterous use of chopsticks
called forth nods of approval, and they began to feel that
their nationality had been definitely established despite
their foreign clothes.

It was dawn and the cocks were crowing when the caval-
cade at last halted at the house of the headman at Onaga
village. The last part of the way the weary strangers had
been carried in bamboo palanquins and were now allowed
to rest. At another house in the neighborhood they were
questioned throughout the following night.

Living quarters were prepared for them at the house of
the village headman, whose wife and children had been
moved across the street. A bamboo fence was then built
around the converted dwelling.

On the fourth morning Manjiro and his friends were
escorted to the house at which their earlier investigation
had taken place. Here Satsuma officials in long silk gowns,
served by an attendant carrying a long spear, continued
their interrogations. Rotating officials from the capital
came frequently thereafter, while native Ryukyuans acted
in turn as resident guards.

After their list of personal questions had been exhausted,
the officials turned their attention to the strangers' boat.
Every item of the cargo was examined and inventoried.
Manjiro's books received special attention, though neither
the printed words nor the tables and diagrams of the texts
on surveying and navigation had any meaning for the examiners. Manjiro did his best to explain, but became
exasperated and visibly nervous when nothing but uncom-
prehending stares or derisive laughter met his efforts.

Perceiving his agitation, the senior official drew him aside
and advised him to calm himself. He then told of a shipwrecked native of Sendai who, having escaped from Russia,
had killed himself when unable to endure the severity of

his trial at the hands of the Japanese. This man's kindly attitude was heartening and gave Denzo an opportunity to add his own word of caution when they had returned to their quarters. Manjiro, he felt, was too impulsive. They must always be humble in an effort to convince their examiners that they were victims of the sea and not runaways.

When they had overcome their self-consciousness at being constantly watched—a routine that seemed mere form— the three friends lost their fear of the immediate future. Food prepared for them at the house across the street was excellent, and they were provided with suitable clothing and given much needed mosquito nets.

Considering the bamboo fence a barrier behind which they must remain without question, Denzo and Goemon made little attempt at intercourse with the islanders. But Manjiro, always restless and friendly, occasionally squirmed through the flimsy barricade and held long conversations in a near-by Mandarin orange grove. He found little difficulty in learning to speak the corrupt native language but did not believe it would be useful on his return to Japan— *if he ever reached that land so long desired!* He seized every opportunity to perfect his Japanese, and he gave special attention to polite phrases used by officials in addressing one of higher rank.

When tug of war contests were held between young men calling themselves East and West teams, he joined the East division and danced with joy when his side won. It was as exciting as baseball games he had watched in Fairhaven.

But he was occasionally melancholy, and his new friends asked the cause. "I lost my father when I was very young," Manjiro replied, "I have just my mother left and I want to see her again. I returned this far at the risk of my life in order to find her. My fate is uncertain, so I weep."

He felt the sympathy of his listeners as they tried to console him. They, and the people generally, were noticeably timid, seemingly ruled by an absent authority whom they feared but must obey. Their inherent kindness was touching.

Four months elapsed, then seven, without any indication that the waiting men would be allowed to return to Japan. Then suddenly they were notified that they were to prepare for a voyage from which they would not return. This was the word they had longed for, yet it brought new apprehension. "If a message does not come from me you will know I have been killed," Manjiro told a sympathetic villager.

On leaving Onaga the trio was carried in palanquins and accompanied by mounted officials with the usual spear men heading the procession. Unrestrained sorrow was expressed by the villagers as they poured out of their thatched dwellings to witness the departure. The headman accompanied them to the boundary of his district, and when last seen was bowing. A strange civilization this, which, knowing nothing of its history, they could not explain.

Darkness shrouded the port of Naha when they arrived. They were taken at once to a Japanese ship lying in the inner harbor and the following morning discovered that the *Adventurer* was already on the high deck. The sea was rough and the captain delayed sailing. Manjiro was surprised at his timidity but wisely made no comment.

Extensive fortifications plainly visible from the ship gave evidence of preparations against attack from the sea. The newcomers had no inkling of the fear that had been growing at this exposed port since the arrival of a French ship demanding trade and other indications of foreign interest in the islands. Nor could they know that such developments, viewed with apprehension by both Ryukyu officials and their overlord Shimadzu (Nariakira) in Japan, had fortuitously shaped to aid them.*

---

* Although unaware of the fact in his lifetime, an American sea

captain had helped to soften the impact of the West on the Ryukyu Islands. Arriving in the harbor of Naha little more than a month before Manjiro's *Adventurer,* and two years prior to Commodore Perry's first contact there, Captain George E. Welch, commanding the bark *Merlin,* was received with kindness and allowed to repair his disabled ship. The charge had been less than $10.00. Elsewhere, the captain testified in Honolulu, the cost would have been more than $1,000.

When the repairs were completed the captain was ordered to leave the harbor. But before weighing anchor he addressed a letter to the authorities. This was an expression of courtesy and Yankee firmness seldom equaled. His letter, published in *The Friend* for February 1851, is scarcely known today, although it is properly a part of the diplomatic correspondence of mid-nineteenth century. The full letter appears in the Appendixes.

15

The Lord of Satsuma

THERE existed at that time a curious and unevenly divided system of government, which Manjiro and his friends did not understand. It had begun six centuries before when the Emperors, devoted to a contemplation of Buddhism and a development of the arts, had allowed their governing power to slip into the hands of the Fujiwara, a noble family which, like the Emperors, claimed divine descent.

As they became luxury-loving and incompetent, a new military clique grew up and finally became dominant. During a war between contending families the Fujiwara fell. Now the victorious Minamoto chief became dictator of the empire. From the Emperor he received the title *Seii Tai-Shogun,* or Barbarian-repressing Generalissimo. This became no empty title, for with the military forces of the empire at his command, each successive Shogun ruled with almost complete authority.

The Tokugawa family had come into power in the sixteenth century. The Shogunate it established was still in control with headquarters at Yedo, some three hundred miles away from the old capital at Kyoto. So powerful and impressive was the Tokugawa Shogunate that the Emperor at Kyoto was almost completely pushed into the background. A descendant of the gods, "held too sacrosanct for human eyes to behold," he was never seen outside his own palace, and had become shadowed in myth.

Actually a vassal of the Emperor, a usurper no higher in rank than some of the daimyo, or feudal lords, who were forced to pay him tribute, and to live part of each year at Yedo, the Shogun was the real ruler.

But Shinto scholars delving into ancient records had stirred almost forgotten loyalties, and among an intellectual minority it was whispered that the true source of power lay in the Emperor.

Lord Shimadzu, with whom Manjiro and his companions dealt first on the southern island of Kyushu, was whole-heartedly in sympathy with the new trend toward recognition of the Emperor. One of the most powerful of the feudal lords, Shimadzu was looking to the future by strengthening the resources of his own fief. The military might of the Shogun must, he reasoned, be met with more military might. The training of warriors and the encouragement of scientific studies under Dutch teachers were steps toward the eventual overthrow of Tokugawa domination. It would not come easily, but restoration of the Divine Rule was worth any sacrifice.

Lord Shimadzu was well aware of the threat of foreign invasion. The Dutch had warned of it, and news seeping in from China through trading junks proved that powerful enemies were abroad. His experiences with a foreign ship* in his own harbor of Kagoshima had convinced him that after two centuries of undisturbed peace Japan was ill prepared. He distrusted friendly advances and had ordered the full force of his shore batteries against the unarmed invaders, with satisfactory results. The hated foreigners had been driven away. But their ship was obviously superior to any he had seen, and the ease with which it maneuvered

---

* The U. S. brig *Morrison*.

beyond the range of his guns was surprising. Japan surely needed new techniques in construction, but how to gain them without loss of face? Japan must never bow to creatures below the notice of the Divine Country. Both the Tokugawa and those bent on driving them from power shared Shimadzu's determination. Japan seethed with internal dissension and yet was united in its resolution to resist impudent foreigners.

Reports from the Ryukyu capital had changed the tenor of Shimadzu's thoughts. Within easy reach—even then on his way to him—was one of his own nationals, a man called Manjiro from the neighboring island province of Tosa, who had traveled in many countries. Perhaps, thought Lord Shimadzu, here was a development come to aid his patriotic cause. The man was of low station, but what matter? He must be encouraged to tell all he had observed.

Delayed by variable winds and poor navigation, the little tribute ship did not reach its destination until the twelfth day after leaving the Ryukyu port of Naha. Each slow mile had brought alternate hope and despair. Many times Manjiro rehearsed a meeting with his mother. *But was she alive? Or had she been forced to suffer beyond endurance for his forbidden departure?* He must know at all costs. "It is dark at the foot of a lighthouse" ran an ancient proverb. . . .

When the little vessel docked at the port of Yamakawa, the returning men were still some miles from Kagoshima, the capital of Satsuma province. They reached the larger port the following day by a coastal ship to which both passengers and Manjiro's whaleboat had been transferred. It was night when they were led ashore and taken to clan headquarters which apparently had been prepared for them.

Paper, tobacco, towels—of such luxuries they had not dreamed! Nor of food and sake! They were sure that spies watched them constantly, but officials who came to question them, while missing no opportunity to probe deeply into their private lives, were not menacing. At times they seemed almost like friends.

Suddenly, without warning, Manjiro was told that an order had come from the palace called *Tsuramakugo*. Lord Shimadzu wished to see him and he was to appear in his foreign clothes. The great lord himself! But why only Manjiro? His friends waited in suspense.

Manjiro never described the magnificence of the castle. To learn the meaning of his call, to steel himself to the ordeal ahead, was apparently all-engrossing and details escaped him. With his need came courage.

When Manjiro was ushered into his presence, Lord Shimadzu dismissed all attendants with a snap of his fan and addressed himself directly to his visitor. He desired to know about the country called America.

To his own surprise Manjiro replied without fear. In America, he said, the people were not graded according to hereditary rank, but were respected for their personal character and ability. Japan's feudal state was poor by comparison. In America there was opportunity for every man, and the nation prospered because each worked for his own advancement as well as the common good. Ambition took the place of fear, good will of class hatred.

How about the barbarian steamships? asked the lord. Why were they so powerful, so swift? Was it true that some ran by hidden power without sails? Seemingly this was the subject uppermost in his mind. Over food and sake the two talked at length. When Manjiro left the castle it was with an order to make a model of an American whale ship.

The model completed, a ship of sufficient size to carry freight around Kagoshima Bay was demanded. This was a disconcerting order for Manjiro, but with the help of a large corps of native carpenters, working at top speed from daylight to dark, and such assistance as Denzo and Goemon could give, the boat was completed in forty-eight days. They often longed for Toraemon and his skill as a builder of boats. Manjiro proposed the name *Ottosen* (Transport) and it was painted on the stern, an innovation in Japanese maritime practice. Great crowds gathered to witness the maiden voyage around the bay. Many cast approving glances at the strange builders, and all three felt a sense of personal achievement.

Powerful as Lord Shimadzu was, he could not longer retain the trio in his custody. Soon after their arrival he had reported by swift runners and clan ship to the inner Tokugawa Council at Yedo, known as the Bakufu, explaining in defense of the Ryukyu officials that the strangers would not have been allowed to land had they come in a ship. Their small boat had not been detected until the men had landed. Their testimony had been taken and a thorough examination of their possessions made. Checked at Kagoshima, the Ryukyu report appeared in good order. There had been no indication that they were Christian proselytes.

A reply now received from the capital took the form of a peremptory order. The men were to be sent to Nagasaki at once. This was the time they had dreaded. Preparations for the journey were hastily made, and, to their surprise, each of the three was given new Japanese clothing and a piece of gold. To a relay of tattooed, muscle-hardened men fell the task of carrying the *Adventurer* and the personal baggage of the prisoners. Three days and three nights later they arrived at Koda village situated on a swift river. Six miles downstream they found two boats waiting in the open sea. Into one with a raised central platform decorated with the Satsuma crest—a cross within a bold circle, typifying the bit ring of a bridle—went the passengers and accompanying officials; guards and baggage were stowed in the other. They then proceeded northwest and five days later were in the crowded harbor of Nagasaki. Here the Satsuma insignia apparently gave them right of way. They were soon at a jetty where they were taken into custody by grim-faced guards.

16

Nagasaki Trials

MANJIRO, Denzo and Goemon knelt before the tribunal. With their heads lowered to the cobblestones and resting on their outstretched hands, they could have had no comprehension of the scene around them. In the silence all they heard was the beating of their hearts.

An eternity it seemed before a droning voice began a recital of their allegiance to the Lord of Tosa, their departure from Usaura, their failure to return from the usual fishing grounds, the fact that after ten years they had reported at the Ryukyus. Now they must reavow their loyalty to *Dai Nippon* and tell what they had seen and heard abroad. They must also explain the circumstances in which one of their number had died.

Were they equipped with a fishing permit and the customary *omamori*, the fisherman's talisman? Maki, lord of Shima and governor of Nagasaki, spoke, addressing himself to Denzo, the senior member of the group.

Assured that all necessary precautions against disaster had been taken, the governor began a gruelling test of Denzo's memory. Often confused as to dates, for now he thought in terms of the Western calendar, Denzo was occasionally assisted by his brother.

The governor was following a course he apparently considered logical. He wished first to know everything possible
about the Sandwich Islands, which, he had been informed,
lay closest to Japan.

The islands, the brothers reported, were several in number. Their harbors were important stopping places for ships
belonging to many countries. Who owned them appeared to
be a disputed question. If America should claim them England would object, and if England took possession, another
country would claim a prior right. They therefore had a
flag which was a combination of the ensigns of several
countries and remained independent.

All of the islands were mountainous; the soil was sandy
and so they produced no grains. Some flat places were given
to farming, but there was no extensive agriculture such as
was found in Japan. Watermelons, gourds, taro, sweet potatoes, millet and bananas were grown. The climate was so
favorable that crops came up all the year around. The
natives did not use hoes, but tilled the soil by sticking it
with a swordlike tool.

Oahu produced no material for clothing, so the people
obtained it by exchanging their products when ships from
China, France, England and other countries entered the
port.

The native women made it their business to wash clothing for seamen. Women of the lower classes also earned a
livelihood by weaving leaves into hats or floor coverings,
while those of higher position remained idle.

On the island on which they lived the wind blew in the
direction of the Ox and the Tiger.

Simplicity was the rule in the islands. The best people
despised liquor as dirt, but many natives chewed a kind of
root which made them sleepy.

Once a sea captain had brought a Japanese sword to
Honolulu. Its keen blade and beautifully decorated hilt

convinced the people that Japan was a land of valor, Denzo declared proudly.

The limits of his ability to explain many matters were soon reached, though he and his brother were often recalled and new testimony taken.

Then Manjiro became the target of the questioners and there was a rustle in the court. Though he lacked a full understanding of many subjects, he had observed carefully, and the information which he was able to give them makes a remarkable record in spite of his limited Japanese and the fact that it was taken down by men completely ignorant of what he was describing.

In an attempt to establish his standing abroad, he drew forth the passport which he had kept concealed in his clothing. Now he explained that this was an official document drawn by a representative of the American government having full authority, and that the raised seal was a mark of office.

It was soon evident that the governor, like Lord Shimadzu, sought information on the new ships. Did they go, as had been reported, by some magic of fire, and was their speed as fast as ocean currents?

In the simplest terms Manjiro reported:

> In the hold of a ship they make a fire. Steam is given off from a boiling cauldron and this turns a motor which causes wheels on both sides of the ship to revolve. The ship then runs on the sea as fast as flying. This is called a steamship. I can find nothing to compare with it.
>
> There is another invention which runs on the land and is called a railroad. They have an iron box about thirteen feet square containing fire which creates steam. This fills the box and then issues out through an iron pipe. The construction is like that of a steamship. [The engine] is fol-

lowed by twenty-three or four iron boxes chained
together, on top of which the cargo is placed, and
within which the passengers sit. These boxes have
two or three windows with glass panes. When one
looks through them when the train is in motion
its swiftness is so great that all objects appear
obliquely and are seen only for an instant. When
possible the route chosen is along flat ground,
avoiding the mountains. This land ship runs on
iron rails.

It is not surprising that Manjiro had difficulty in explaining the telegraph since Morse, the inventor, had long been
an object of ridicule, and only eight years previously the
first message, "What hath God wrought?" had been flashed
from the Supreme Court in Washington to Baltimore. This
had but deepened the mystery for the general public. Manjiro seems to have vaguely grasped the idea of an electro-
magnetic principle. He reported:

It uses a wire stretched high above the road and
the letter hung on it goes from one station to another without the aid of a messenger. To prevent
the letter from colliding with another they use a
device which I do not understand. I think the
letter is drawn by a magnet iron.

A merchant being low in the social scale, it was in order
for Manjiro to be questioned concerning the source of his
wealth. Had he ever engaged in business? No, Manjiro
answered, all the money he had ever earned was by work
of his hands. What about his watch? It was much too pre-
tentious for a fisherman's son. There was also a grave matter concerning firearms found among his things.

Even children, Manjiro replied, carried watches in
America. He had brought his for his own convenience, not
for unseemly display. And as for firearms, they were a

necessity, especially in California where life was rugged. On the subject of the United States Manjiro dwelled with delight:

The country is about 6,930 American miles from east to west, and about 4,100 miles from north to south. It is divided into states. It was founded by Englishmen but does not belong to England. Some Englishmen use it as a trading post. The capital is New York.

Being in thirty to fifty degrees north, the air is clear and pure and the climate very regular in both warm and cold seasons, causing grain to thrive. The climate of New England is like that of Japan.

The American government is said to be the best in the world. The magistrate is chosen from the people for his talent and learning. His stay in office is limited to four years, but if he excels in virtue and good administration he is not let go after four years. He is given a pension when he retires. Talented men from all over the country compete for this high office.

The present magistrate is called Taylor* and he is said to be just in law and punishment. There was a war with Mexico over a border question and he led the attacking army to a great victory, by which he won many honors and was at last made magistrate.

He lives very simply and goes about on horseback, followed by a single retainer. Officials are hard to distinguish as they never display the authority of their office. They do not demand courtesies from citizens along the road.

There is no distinction between classes. Even a man of low rank may become an official. There

---

* News of President Taylor's death had been received at Honolulu while Manjiro was preparing to sail but had apparently not been communicated to him.

is no restriction on the amount of land a man may own and he is taxed according to his resources. A tax is taken on each head. For a boy fifteen years of age it is one silver [dollar].

The natives are perfect in body, with white skins. Some of them are six feet tall. They are naturally gentle and sympathetic and prize integrity and chivalry. Above all, they are industrious and trade with countries in all directions.

More than fifty years before its actual accomplishment, Manjiro told the insular Japanese of international hopes for the Panama Canal. Many times he had heard the subject discussed and was aware that such a waterway would not only do away with hazardous and dreary passages around Cape Horn, but would change the relations of the whole world. He told of the engineering difficulties:

North and South America are connected by only a small strip of land, the narrowest part of which has a width of some five leagues. If this could be cut through it would be a source of great convenience and profit to navigation. The project has been delayed because of the objection that the tide on the Pacific side being higher, and there being a fountain of tide there, the water would rush into the Gulf of Mexico and inundate the land.

When the subject of ships recurred, Manjiro had the chance he had been waiting for. His own experience in traveling long distances at sea with greatly reduced supplies—plus long talks with his benefactor in Honolulu—had impressed him with the need to speak boldly. He gave the facts in his own way:

American ships entering ports of Japan have been ordered to leave immediately, and compelled to do so without accomplishing any results. When a whale ship or a trading ship is delayed by a storm there is a shortage of water and fuel. The Americans seek permission to get these things and if necessary would be willing to leave a hostage. In spite of their humble proposals, the Japanese made a great commotion, to the astonishment of the Americans. Such stories have been reported in detail. The Americans are better tempered than the Japanese. Their country being opened, they have no desire to annex any other country. In sailing from California to China a ship is carrying so many pasengers and such a quantity of goods that it is impossible to load enough provisions. The distance between America and China being something like fifteen hundred *ri,* it is impossible to make the long voyage back to California to get coal when it has run short. So I understand that they want to get a storage place for coal in Satsuma, Nippon. I read this report when I was in Oahu last year in a newspaper called *Friend.**

Tension was relieved when Manjiro spoke of the heavenly bodies he had come to know by name. He reported a north polar star, but none at the South Pole.

His examiners were surprised to learn that the Milky Way, to their teaching the river of the sky, extended to other parts of the world. They eagerly inquired whether from America he could observe the *katsura* bush, which they thought they could see growing on the face of the moon. His report of fire on the sea called phosphorescence, over which his ship had passed safely, was not explained by their legendary "Dragon's Light" and its truth was questioned.

More than once Manjiro's face burned as he was plied

---

* Further recorded testimony appears in the Appendixes.

with questions concerning his private life. He was repeatedly warned by the cautious Denzo that words spoken in anger would only make matters more difficult for them all. Thus far they had been remarkably well treated and should feel thankful.

They were prepared for the ceremony which came at the end of the eighteenth period of questioning when a court attendant took from a box a metal plate embossed with the crucifixion scene. They all remembered the *fumiyé* from a number of years before when every villager throughout the realm had been required to place his feet on it as proof that he had not accepted the Catholic religion. As established procedure, it was now quickly accomplished.*

They had all hoped that the end of their detention might be near, but now their guards were ordered to return them to prison. Manjiro's anger flared as they were again led through narrow streets to the foreign-looking stone building at the place called Sakuramachi. If not the same prison in which the *Lagoda* crewmen had been incarcerated, it was indeed similar. The cagelike cells were too low to permit standing upright, too dark to see clearly. The description Manjiro had read in Honolulu fitted perfectly. With none but his friends and the prison guards to hear, he made no effort to restrain his temper. He felt, it appears, like a carp fighting its way upstream, suddenly blocked from further progress. He had reached the limit of his endurance.

Suddenly a half-familiar voice halted his tirade. "Are you Manjiro?" it asked. "And where is Denzo?" It was the leader of the shipwrecked group from Kishu which they had attempted to join in Honolulu. The five had at last reached their homeland through China, and were waiting to learn

---

* In later years Manjiro told his sons that men grasping both his arms propelled him over the image set on the floor.

their fate. They all huddled together for a while and talked in whispers. Nervous exhaustion finally forced Manjiro to sleep.

When he awoke on the cold floor, a world of beauty seemed to have unfolded. Itinerant ballad singers, *Joruri,* were performing in the dark street below. Perhaps for the first time Manjiro the fisherman was hearing the classic romance *Osome Hisamatsu* and the famous story, *"Shigure no Kotatsu,"* "The Hearth and the Rain." The phrasing was poetic. Its emotional overtures stirred his long-dormant imagination and brought him strange peace.

They were held there for three days longer. Unknown to them, their fortunes had changed. The trials had ended with a favorable report to the Bakufu. Manjiro's books had been examined by Dutch translators, and final confirmation of their place of birth and the circumstances surrounding their shipwreck had been received from the record office in their home province. A delegation had already been sent by Yamanouchi Toyoshige, the lord of Tosa, to receive them.

In preparation for their release, the men were given new clothes and told to shave their heads as evidence of Japanese ancestry. Manjiro had hoped to go before his mother looking like an American. Long after his pompadour was off he instinctively reached to smooth it. The stiff topknot tied with paper string and brought forward over his partly shaved head seemed a poor substitute.

In the ceremony of dismissal the governor sat on the elevated platform in the great audience hall, with lesser officials ranged on lower levels according to rank. All wore ceremonial garments of stiff silk, with short swords in their girdles, their long swords on the floor beside them. The Tosa official sat at the end of the row; his assistants knelt in the courtyard.

The release was read in the singsong voice the prisoners had come to know:

This is to certify that Denzo, his younger brother Goemon, of Usaura, Takaoka-gun in the province of Tosa, territory of Matsudaira of Tosa, and Manjiro of Nakanohama, Hata-gun, were stranded on a desert island in the Year of the Ox, were rescued by a foreign ship, lived abroad for some years and returned to Ryukyu. Upon examination at this office as to their lives abroad, they are proven innocent of having been converted to the sect of Christianity and other evil report; in short, they are worthy to be returned to their native province.

It is imperative that they should not live hereafter outside of said province unless called by the government at Yedo, and that we should be notified in case of their death.

Articles acquired or purchased abroad, such as gold dust, coins, gold, silver, copper, guns, bullets, drugs, navigation instruments, foreign dice and also their boat and tackle are retained. Japanese silver pieces are granted in exchange for the gold dust and foreign coins.

This notice referred to and authorized by the Yedo Government (Bakufu).

The reading finished, the three prisoners were required to impress the tips of their inked fingers over their names on the document.

With the return home so near, Manjiro did not openly grieve over the confiscated whaleboat and other personal treasures. The gold nugget he had hoped to give his mother, Bowditch's *Navigator,* a history of the United States, a *Life* of George Washington, an arithmetic and dictionary, a text on letter writing, a farmer's almanac and most of his maps were his greatest loss. *He had bought them with his own money or friends had given them to him. Might they not be given back?* He could not answer the question he often asked himself.

Leaving Nagasaki harbor under favorable winds, the ship, resplendent with Tosa emblems, headed for the home island of Shikoku. On leaving Nagasaki the wayfarers doubtless saw fan-shaped Deshima, the island in the harbor where Dutch traders were forced to live. But as at Ryukyu, in the case of Dr. Bettleheim, they had never been allowed to meet them.

17

Manjiro Meets His Mother

HOME at last! Yet the three friends were still denied dear familiar sights. In Kochi, the capital, they must first take care of the formalities relating to men who had broken the law by leaving the country. Despite the Nagasaki record, the officials did their best to find serious flaws in the culprits' testimony. Not so familiar with cases like this, they apparently sought to outdo the Nagasaki inquisitors.

Villagers gathered in the streets were not allowed to catch a glimpse of their fellow provincials until this last trial was over. Meanwhile they were detained at an inn which had been barricaded in advance of their arrival.

Then came an order for Manjiro to dress in his foreign clothes to make a visit to relatives of Lord Yamanouchi at their villa. About Manjiro's age, and perhaps uncertain of his proper role, the lord had sanctioned the call. When his curiosity had been satisfied by this indirect means, Lord Yamanouchi forthwith issued an order granting the three men life pensions of rice. They would thus be enabled to live in simple comfort, though they were still deprived of their fishing rights.

With feelings of profound relief, the three set out for Usaura sixty miles away. Denzo's house was no longer standing, and so they went to the home of his cousin who welcomed them joyfully. Apparently content to resume the old village routine, the brothers never again figured in Manjiro's life.

After an overnight rest, Manjiro proceeded alone to Nakanohama. He fulfilled his most pressing obligation by calling first on the village headman. News of his arrival at the capital had preceded him, and curious people surrounded the house. Suddenly the crowd parted. Manjiro's mother came forward. For a breathless moment she gazed at her son, so changed, yet with a light in his eyes that revealed deep filial affection. With the reserve demanded of a widowed mother, she tremulously inquired his name. Then she covered her face with her hands and burst into uncontrollable sobs. Manjiro held back the often-rehearsed words of endearment. His role as the head of his mother's house demanded dignity. His long absence and the presence of strangers helped to sustain an air of formality. "*Okāsan*— Mother!" he said simply in a choked voice.

When the crowd had dispersed, mother and son walked silently side by side along the road and through the familiar gate. Then, in a few moments alone, they experienced the real joy of reunion. Her son had traveled more than miles, the mother could see, but the old bond was there; it had never been broken. "*Arigatai! Arigatai!*" she said softly, expressing highest thankfulness.

Soon neighbors trooped in, bearing gifts of fish, the traditional red beans cooked with rice and congratulatory cups of sake. Manjiro's brothers and sisters, grown almost beyond his recognition, waited on the guests. In an interval of quiet they pointed out to him a tomb adjoining the village temple which, thinking him dead, their mother had erected to his memory. Counting the date of his departure as that of his death, she had observed the anniversary each year as a memorial day.

According to custom, she had adopted a son so that the

house might not be without a responsible head. Now he participated cheerfully in the joyous welcome. It was late when all the visitors had gone and brothers and sisters were asleep. Long into the night mother and son talked fitfully with deep content.

Three days and three nights Manjiro remained at his old home. He was then summoned to Kochi and learned that Lord Yamanouchi had decided that his most-talked-of vassal might well be employed in teaching foreign ways. He was given the status of a low-class samurai and presented with the customary sword. Manjiro considered a display of arms in broad daylight foolish and unnecessary and often disguised his sword with a towel, as though he were carrying the long roots of *gobo* used for food. He wanted always to be known as a man of peace.

But he was not without honor in his own province. In its more relaxed atmosphere he was at his unassuming best. Here he not only reiterated what he had told under duress in Nagasaki, but in private conversation pictured features of Western life in marked contrast to those he had observed since returning home. To many he was known as *Sensei Sama,* Honorable Teacher. Many times he was asked to decorate private fans with the queer sideways writing of the barbarians.

He also conducted classes for those with a thirst for the new knowledge. These had been cleared by the clan office and included some men destined for important roles in a drama yet unforeseen by the nation. In place of a blackboard Manjiro made a chart which contained the twenty-six English letters and hung it in the *tokonoma* before which his pupils sat on the matted floor. As he gave the pronunciation, his pupils laboriously copied each letter with the brush and inkstone which they habitually carried in their kimono sleeves. Strange offshoot of a New England school! And revolutionary in remote Tosa where even Dutch influence had but slightly penetrated!*

When Manjiro spread out his one remaining map of the world (made in England in 1846 and said to be the latest anywhere in the country) there was intense excitement. Where, a fourteen-year-old boy named Goto Shojiro inquired, was Japan? Manjiro remembered what Captain Whitfield had told him when he asked the same question. He indicated the area on the map and replied that their country appeared only as a group of small dots on the broad expanse of the Pacific Ocean.

Hearing of this map and convinced that it would be of great value to the government,† Lord Yamanouchi ordered Kawada Shoryu,‡ his most talented artist, to copy it with place names in Japanese supplied by Manjiro. Many scholars came to follow the progress of the work. Kawada, the artist, became so interested that, in Manjiro's absence, he occasionally essayed the role of instructor; he never tired of pointing out sections of the globe he was learning to call by their English names. Western forms of government interested him greatly.

---

* It is still related in Tosa that one of Manjiro's pupils, learning to pronounce a word signifying an article of Western masculine wearing apparel, was on his way home from school when he stumbled and fell into a ditch. Pulled out in a dazed condition by a passer-by, he mumbled the word *shirt* instead of the customary thanks.

† Foreign maps were a source of great interest, but woe to the man who gave a map of Japan to a foreigner! Von Siebold, an early Dutch physician, learned the consequences when the official astronomer gave him maps in exchange for Russian books and a map of New Holland (Australia). These the astronomer hoped to duplicate for the benefit of his government. When his guilt was established, he took his life by the honorable method of hara-kiri, and von Siebold was banished from the country.

‡ It was this man who set down Manjiro's story in the four volumes translated in the Brooklyn Museum and copied for this writer.

18

An Important Call

TATTOOED runners had arrived in Kochi. The dispatch box they carried bore the trefoil crest of Tokugawa. Soon Kochi throbbed with excitement. There was a crisis at the Shogun's capital, and Manjiro was needed there. So that he could speak with those in authority when he reached Yedo, Lord Yamanouchi raised his rank. The message from the capital had been worded politely, but the Lord of Tosa immediately sent back apologies for not having been more liberal in bestowing honors on his most prominent citizen.

Manjiro had secured a house in Kochi and had expected to have his mother live with him. Thus far she had refused, saying that she was a country woman and would find it hard to be at home in the more sophisticated life of the city. She was proud of her son, but the light of his achievements would reach her at any distance. Now, before he could communicate with her, he was on his way to the seat of government on Honshu, the main island of Japan.

Tosa was the center of its own island world and was not yet fully aware of the significance of the events that were responsible for Manjiro's call to Yedo. Everywhere the news of a foreign invasion was spreading, yet its full meaning could not at once be grasped. A powerful barbarian called Commodore Perry had suddenly appeared in Uraga

Bay with fabulous fire ships. In the name of the President of the United States, he announced, he had come to demand better treatment of shipwrecked sailors and the right to purchase supplies for foreign ships. It was as if an apparition had suddenly appeared in the sky. There was rumor of invasion and there was fear of immediate destruction by the huge guns so plainly visible from the shore. Dread of barbarian magic had increased the apprehension of the people who, moved by a common impulse, sought the hills in great crowds and built beacon fires to warn the countryside. Rockets lighted the sky, and temple bells tolled.

Shore batteries discharged their guns seemingly without effect as the big ships continued to move farther into Uraga Bay. A convulsive shudder ran through the multitude on the shore when the nine-o'clock gun was fired from the flagship. All the occupants of a guard boat in the harbor jumped overboard in their fright. Worse still, that fearsome first night, was the appearance of a meteor, a large blue sphere with a red wedge-shaped tail. It lighted the heavens until four o'clock the following morning and was clearly a sign of the gods' displeasure.

The uproar had soon reached the capital at Yedo. Small boats brought breathless messengers who repeated awesome tales.

> In all directions were seen mothers flying with children in their arms and men with mothers on their backs. Rumors of an immediate invasion, exaggerated each time they were communicated from mouth to mouth, added horror to the horror-stricken. The tramp of war horses, the clatter of armed warriors, the noises of carts, the parade of firemen, the incessant tolling of bells, the shrieks of women, the cries of children, dinning all the streets of more than a million souls made confusion confounded.

Thus a Japanese historian described it.*

At first Perry had been remote. He had declared that the ruler whose credentials he bore was equal to the Emperor in rank and had remained in his cabin while his officers carried on preliminary business. Finally, despite vacillating officials and enforced delays, he had gone ashore amid thunderous salutes from his ships.

Knowing full well that he was dealing with the most ceremonious people on earth, Perry proceeded to stretch military display to a point at which it would be impressive to all and sundry. In a highly dramatized ceremony the American President's letter, encased in a magnificent gold box with outer covering of rosewood hinged with gold, was formally delivered. When the commodore spoke, it was firmly, as one accustomed to command. He would leave the letter, he said, and return in the spring for an answer. *And when he returned he would probably bring more ships.*

It had been effectively and decisively done. There was no mistaking either what the demands were or how they would be carried out. In the reigning confusion one thing was agreed on in the councils of the Bakufu: The impudent barbarians must be kept out of Yedo, for there the true nature of the dual government would be disclosed and they would discover that the letter they carried with such aplomb had not been addressed to the ruler in power. In consternation, and for the first time in over two centuries of military supremacy, the Bakufu had notified the banished Emperor of the national calamity.† Prayers beseech-

---

* The late Dr. Inazo Nitobe.

† Wrote the historian, F. Brinkley: "A more signal abrogation of autocratic power could not have been effected. The Shogun thereby virtually abdicated his position as the nation's administrative sovereign and placed himself on a level with all the territorial nobles who had hitherto been required to render implicit obedience to his orders."

ing safety and wisdom were said before the sacred inner shrine at Ise and other important centers of worship.

In such a crisis the advice of scholars outweighed the prognostications of ancient astrologers. One Otsuki Bankei, known for his advancement in Dutch studies, particularly commanded respect. He it was who reported that a man known as Manjiro, recently on trial at Nagasaki, had first-hand information of the barbarians. He had lived in their country and knew what manner of men they were. Moreover, he had correctly described their steamships in advance of the squadron's arrival. Why not bring him to Yedo to report further? Why not indeed? the Bakufu agreed. He might have information of real value.

In such unprecedented circumstances Manjiro had been called. On such slender hopes did the highest in the land await the arrival of a commoner. Or had they conveniently forgotten that he was a fisherman's son?

19

On the Way to Yedo

MANJIRO reached the old capital of Kyoto through the port of Osaka. There he entered a waiting *kago* or palanquin to be borne over the Tokaido, the great highway stretching three hundred miles to the seat of the Shogun's government at Yedo. Doubtless his summons filled him with apprehension. What did the great Shogun want of him? Was he to be disgraced and beheaded, or merely commanded to tell again—this time to the highest in the land—the nature of the strange world into which a tempest had blown him? He had left Japan against his wish, and thus far no extreme penalty had been exacted. But what would the mighty ruler think, what punishment meted out, now that the barbarian country he had represented as friend had sent armed ships to force an unwilling promise?

But Manjiro had heard only the vague rumor and had no knowledge of political implications. To his mind international trade was not only desirable but relatively simple. He had observed it in operation, and his American friends had foreseen its benefits to Japan. Too, he was young and had known nothing of terror since some twelve years before, when, in sight of the graves of similar victims of shipwreck, he had faced starvation.

It was the season known in New England as Indian

Summer and in Japan as Little Spring—a glorious season for travel. Ahead stretched a road of wondrous beauty which had been built centuries before by artisans combining an inherent love of nature with amazing skill. The elevated portions of this highway had been paved with stones passed from hand to hand, now worn smooth by incessant travel. Seldom many miles out of sight of the sea, the road was protected from its ravages by earthen embankments on which grew venerable pine trees, twisted and bent by the capricious hand of nature. Almost unreal in its beauty, it opened a new world to a traveler who had never before been privileged to see his own country in its infinite variety.

The Seven Grasses of Autumn, part of his boyhood appreciation of natural beauty, grew everywhere along the roadsides. Billowing fields of rice, almost ready for harvest, the darker green of the tea shrub shorn of young leaves, and the higher lands planted to winter wheat—sown in rows, not broadcast as in New England—had the appearance of abundance. But this was not New England with broad acres filling the bins of prosperous farmers. This was Japan wresting from pitifully small plots of land a bare livelihood. Unceasing, backbreaking toil it undoubtedly meant, yet the laborers seemed contented. Everywhere he paused to rest, the stranger was greeted with smiles. As rumors of his shipwreck were whispered about, he saw signs of wonder and delight. This man was of their own heritage. A human controlled by a God, some said, for had he not defied the same elements that had driven him away to return to his beloved country? And was there not meaning in the fact that he had returned in the Year of the Ox, the same in which he had left?

Everywhere the highway presented striking contrasts. Mile-long processions of military retainers, with imposing display, accompanying their feudal lords on their way to pay homage to the Shogun, held undisputed right of way. Orna-

ments carried on long poles were similar to those Manjiro
had seen in Hawaii. They indicated high rank. The pag-
eantry was sharpened by the staccato command, "Be down,"
and the sight of kneeling peasants with foreheads obedi-
ently to the ground as the processions passed. The pompous
arrogance of mounted swordsmen would scarcely have been
unnoticed by a man who had testified to the unpretentious
character of Western officials.

Each district was ruled by a daimyo and had its own
money, good nowhere else; and an exchange of *kinsatsu,*
or money cards, was a requirement at each boundary.
At these points menacing guardhouses displayed imple-
ments of torture, grim warnings to any who might disregard
the law, and in much-traveled areas roofed edict boards
reminded all of the extreme penalty:

> So long as the sun shall warm the earth, let no
> christian be so bold as to come to Japan; and let
> all know that the King of Spain himself, or the
> christian god, or the great God of all, if he violate
> this command, shall pay for it with his head.

The fifty-three post stations provided overnight rests and
hot baths for travelers. Fresh bearers or horses waited at
each station for the next lap of the journey. Every traveler
found it a relief to climb down from the cramped *kago,*
relax and bathe. Every settlement had its community bath-
house. Did Manjiro realize, one wonders, that free discussions at these public gathering places approximated the
Town Meetings which were such an important part of life
in New England? That they were the first stirrings of democracy in his backward country and that the brightly
colored hand-blocked prints called *ukiyo-e*—"the passing
world"—were a first form of a people's newspaper?

Wayside inns presented smoke-filled kitchens to the eyes

of travelers on the road and carefully hid the charm of rear gardens. These walled-in bits of fairyland, with grafted trees, miniature waterfalls and natural stones skillfully placed to reveal tones and values, gave welcome pause during a strenuous journey.

Villages overlapped thickly; each was devoted to its ancestral craft of spinning, weaving, carving, lacquer or pottery making. Manjiro must have noticed with amusement clumsy straw shoes being made for horses and sold along the road. Years later the horses of the American Consul would be borrowed so that their metal shoes could be copied. Manjiro had already tried to tell his people of the Western way of protecting horses' feet.

Torii and long avenues of cryptomeria trees pointed the way to hidden temples, and white-robed pilgrims, each with his supporting staff, created an aura of peace. There were many shrines with approaching steps worn deep by centuries of climbing feet. Often seen was a stone Jizo, friend of travelers and protector of children, his lap full of pebbles carried as votive offerings by bereaved mothers seeking protection for their little ones.

Wild camellias, as tall as trees, were in late bloom—their dark, glossy foliage enhancing the charm of delicate petals. These flowers, as all knew, belonged to the common people. They were never cultivated in gardens of the samurai, for the blossoms did not shed their petals but fell in full glory to the ground, a warning that the professional fighter might lose his head while in the vigor of manhood.

At swift rivers skilled boatmen waited to ferry travelers across. Where distances between banks were short and the water shallow, travelers were carried pickaback, their *kagos* born aloft by coolies trained in the art of balance on slippery stones.

Manjiro surely delighted in the strange and interesting sights among the peasantry. In populous districts the road was filled with food and charcoal vendors, jugglers, wrestlers, snake charmers, peddlers of singing insects, itinerant storytellers wearing rush hats like inverted wastebaskets; others had weird masks that brought to life goblins and beasts of folklore. In all the world there was no busier or merrier scene.

To a swift traveler the great highway was a confused picture. In the distance he could catch intermittent views of winding stream beds, misty waterfalls, forests of feathery bamboo and occasional breath-catching glimpses of Fujiyama, the sacred mountain.

This was the Tokaido of the artist Hiroshige, then still at work on wood-block prints that would one day immortalize his name in every corner of the globe. But with all its novelty and beauty, the journey was often wearisome. Surely Manjiro was in a hurry to reach Yedo, hold what it might of good or ill.

20

In the Capital of the Shogun

When Manjiro reached *Nihon Bashi,* or Great Bridge of Japan, he was at the point from which distances throughout the empire were reckoned. At the heart of a great pulsing city, it spanned the moat spiraling through the center. Canals branched off the principal waterway to the outlying river. Water-borne traffic congested them; the cries of boatmen and the clatter of thousands of wooden clogs in the narrow streets created an incessant roar. To a visitor from the country it was sheer bedlam.

In the inner ring of the great moat, aloof from this plebeian scene, stood the Shogun's castle and surrounding it the *yashiki,* or mansions of the most powerful daimyo, each within a walled compound. The whole region was designed as an impregnable camp, with thick walls of stone rising from the waters of the moat, and innumerable gateways defended by towers with wide embrasures. The outer barracks were manned by the two-sworded samurai and artisans in their employ. Beyond these confines stretched the parade grounds and archery ranges.

Despite the imposing display of military might this vast region had become an effete world, with court life at an extreme pitch of splendor. During enforced periods of residence at the capital, feudal lords and their families took

147

delight in vast pleasure gardens brought to the highest per-
fection of landscape art; in *cha no yu,* the aesthetic ritual of
serving and partaking of ceremonial tea; in flower arrangement and painting. Scenes by renowned artists hung in the
alcoves of the rooms, whose sliding doors had been designed
by others of equal fame. The finest porcelains graced the
low tables. Thus the nobility lived a luxurious, refined life,
devoted to the arts. The samurai, depended on for defense,
gradually lost their vigor. Armor was rusty; warriors were
soft.

Perry's arrival had brought this condition of affairs to
an abrupt halt. It was now mid-October and gloom had
settled over the council chambers of Bakufu. Heroic efforts
to strengthen coast defenses against the return of the American squadron had been in progress for three months. The
Shinagawa forts, a monument to determined energy, were
almost completed. But faith in ancient guns and stone and
earthen emplacements had rapidly declined. The governor
of Uraga, and others who had accompanied him to the
American ships, had reported guns beyond description,
while all had heard deafening roars reverberating through
once tranquil hills. That these had resulted from blank fire
salutes and but hinted at the destructive power of modern
warfare was a point hardly missed.

Manjiro could have known nothing of the prevailing
apprehension, or the reason for the secrecy with which his
arrival was surrounded. At the Yedo headquarters of the
Tosa clan, he received necessary instructions. He had been
called in a national emergency, he was told, and was to be
questioned by representatives of the government who
would have to make some great decisions. His part would
be to serve his country. This was an obligation above all
obligations. That he was constantly watched—that furtive
eyes and ears were behind every screen—was part of a con-

sciousness even more poignant than at Nagasaki where he had not stood alone.

An early caller was a subordinate officer of Abe Masahiro, lord of Ise. Lord Abe was the Prime Minister, member of a family of hereditary Tokugawa retainers. Despite his venerable title, *Tairo* ("Great Old"), he was young, also clever and cautious. He did not trust the barbarians, but he realized that Japan must deal with them, perhaps make some concessions. Already he had stirred up a hornet's nest by sending copies of the American President's letter to the leading daimyo with a request for written opinions. This unprecedented action had weakened the power of the Shogunate, for clan rulers, long required to render implicit obedience, were growing restive for a change of rule. Many were indignant that firmer measures had not at once been taken against the invaders.

A favorable report on Manjiro, the extent of his knowledge and ability to express himself clearly, resulted in an order from Lord Abe for a personal visit. Manjiro further impressed the Prime Minister with his serious demeanor and lack of evasion. A succession of conferences took place at his *yashiki* near the Imperial Palace where trusted associates foregathered. In the circumstances all were willing to overlook Manjiro's ignorance of established etiquette. What he had to tell them was of primary importance.

Among the questioners was Kawaji Toshiakira, a retainer of the Shogunate, who had risen to the position of Minister of Finance. His realistic views were in line with those of the Prime Minister.

Impressive for his good looks and dignified bearing was Hayashi Daigaku no Kami, who listened intently but seldom spoke. His title identified him with the great institution of classical learning of which he was the regent. He was a noted Chinese scholar, a fact weighing heavily in his selection as a commissioner in the forthcoming negotiations. It had been noted that Commodore Perry's chief interpreter could both read and write Chinese, and it was believed that medium would again be used in addition to Dutch, for which the Americans had also made provision.

The clear gaze of Egawa Tarozaemon set him apart from the group as one who earnestly sought light on a difficult situation and would go to any length to find it. He had been chosen to visit the flagship on its return and to speak with the authority vested in him by the Bakufu. Fate was to decree otherwise, but the early meeting of this clearheaded and progressive officer of the Shogunate with the young man who had circumnavigated the earth was to bear fruit in surprising ways. Egawa was a student of the Dutch language and military science, a man of vision and of action. He was directing his energies toward the building of forts,* and ideas for new ship models were already taking shape in his mind. With the early removal of the government ban on construction of ocean-going ships—already a foregone conclusion—interest in Perry's ships and a desire to build similar vessels were stimulating many. Manjiro was the man whose assistance Egawa wanted. He was convinced that Manjiro would make the best possible interpreter and his personal call on Prime Minister Abe was early proof of his confidence in Manjiro's loyalty.

Much depended on the stand taken by Mito Nariaki, lord of Mito. He was a violent dissenter in any discussion relative to opening the ports. Of Tokugawa blood, he was near the top in rank, a member of the "Three Families" from which a successor to the Shogun would be chosen should the main line fail. But in his zest for the scholarship encouraged by his illustrious ancestor, he had explored records of the times when early Emperors had been in power, and his sympa-

---

* The masonry of some of these is still to be seen in Tokyo Bay.

thies had turned toward the banished ruler. No move could be made without his knowledge, yet his rank precluded ordinary contacts.

Letters from the Prime Minister and the high-placed Mito reveal official opinion of the foreigners and are interesting a century later for their impersonal form of address and quaint legendary flavor:

Lord of Ise to Egawa Tarozaemon

JANUARY 23
FIRST YEAR OF ANSEI [lunar calendar]

In the course of our conversation during your visit a little while ago, you related in detail regards Manjiro and explained that, since you are to go aboard the ship to persuade the squadron to turn back, you would be immensely inconvenienced without a person to act as interpreter. As for Manjiro, it was your assurance that, being in a position to fathom his inmost heart, you would take it upon yourself to guarantee that he would never act to the prejudice of the Shogunate. Such being the case, and taking into consideration such a circumstance as might arise at any moment to call you urgently to depart, my hasty conclusion then was to agree to what you had suggested. Afterward, however, I turned the whole matter over in my mind very carefully. There is no reason whatsoever to be apprehensive about your guarantee for things. It is very apparent that Manjiro himself never cherishes a treacherous desire. But foreign motives are difficult to speculate upon. That an unforeseen situation might arise on board the ship in which Manjiro might be taken away with the foreigners is beyond anybody's guarantee. Furthermore, there are persons, among them Grand Lord of Mito, who entertain serious apprehensions. Under the circumstances, in the event that you might be called upon to visit the ship within this night, it is advisable that you refrain from

taking Manjiro with you. It is my intention to take
up the matter at the Castle when I attend there
tomorrow, and let you hear the consequences as
quickly as possible. Everything we do is in the
cause of the Shogun. You are advised to have
patience.

The Lord of Mito to Egawa Tarozaemon

FEBRUARY 2

EGAWA ESQ:

Pleased to know that Egawa is progressing so
well in this cold weather. It is a thousand pities
that the Americans came before even the half-way
was accomplished in the manufacture of guns.
Mito wholeheartedly concurs in the wish that,
even one by one, the guns will be finished with
speed and the ones that are ready fully equipped
with carriages immediately. As regards Manjiro,
Egawa has seen through his heart and found it
clear of all suspicion. Manjiro is to be praised for
yearning so much for home, and eventually coming back. But consider that the Americans took
advantage of Manjiro's youth to separate him
from others and did a favor by teaching writing
and arithmetic. In so doing who can tell that there
was not a doubtful scheme in mind? Manjiro was
saved from death and put under obligation of
gratitude for upbringing from early boyhood to
twenty years of age. That it will not be to Manjiro's liking to do anything to the disadvantage
of the Americans is natural. Therefore even if
Egawa sees well, it would be advisable that all
chances be eliminated of meeting anyone of the
Americans when they come ashore, and that Manjiro be kept in ignorance of secret conferences,
not to mention restrained from going on board the
ships. Depending on how Egawa makes use of the
man, it will help toward enlightenment on the
state of affairs in America, and it is left to Egawa's
good sense and discretion to turn Manjiro into an

instrument to be employed in defense. Though fully relying on Egawa's tactfulness, still apprehension has caused these few lines. Pray excuse this scribble in haste before attending the Castle.

[Signed] THE HERMIT OF MITO

P.S. It will be imprudent, in view of the times, to leave that man loose at pasture, but to make too confined and ill at ease would reduce usefulness. Treat generously, while guarding carefully. There was once a dragon tamed and domesticated that one day drove through wind and cloud in the midst of a hurricane and took flight. Once that man changed his mind and was taken away on an American ship it would be to repent too late.

With regard to dealings with Americans Mito agrees that lacking preparation for defense the Americans should be tactfully persuaded to leave in peace. Once successful, demands will know no bounds. Just like *Kappa* [a legendary river monster], and *Raiju* [a creature connected with the God of Thunder], the Americans are rampant only because of being on water and the strength of fire-arms. Tumbling about in a field, a *Kappa* or a *Raiju* is a mere nothing. Until the time when well prepared with ships and guns, it is hoped that, dealing with those Americans, Nippon will have the high spirit of fighting a hand to hand combat with lightening speed. Mito hopes and believes that Egawa's pluck and courage will not fail to make the invaders' blood run cold. Here Mito takes the opportunity to manifest notorious obstinacy.

The Bakufu found it politic to stand behind the imperious Mito. That Manjiro had been educated to further the Americans' purpose was sound logic, some agreed, and having come ahead of the American squadron, he was quite probably a spy bent on reconnaissance. In any event, as Mito had said, he was too valuable to lose.

As a concession, Manjiro was soon transferred from the Tosa headquarters to Egawa's *yashiki* where it would be possible to go more fully into discussions, every phase of which Egawa was finding provocative of new ideas. He regarded Manjiro's return to Japan as providential; he had come back just in time to be of great service. Though Manjiro could not take part in the official negotiations, he could put his general knowledge to good use.

21

Convention by Remote Control

SHORTLY after he arrived at Yedo, Manjiro was sent under guard to Uraga. Mysterious markings had appeared on the jetty while Perry was presenting the President's letter at neighboring Kurihama the year before. Could Manjiro explain them? He could and did. They were merely the letters of the English alphabet, scrawled, perhaps, by a sailor idly passing the time! Did Manjiro laugh? Or had he learned that there was no mirth for the Bakufu in any situation they could construe as suspicious?

Along the shore he saw thousands of laborers at work on breastworks of earth faced with stone. To him it must have appeared both warlike and futile. For had he not said at Nagasaki, and many times since, that the Americans traded with countries in all directions and that they sought no territory in Japan? *Why prepare to fight them?* Japan, he kept repeating, was the only country in the world refusing trade bounties which all might profitably share.

Commodore Perry's promise to return the following spring was fulfilled on February 12, 1854. His unerring sense of good theater was again in evidence. Spectators lining the shores witnessed a parade of ships which to the simplest man recalled long years of boatbuilding restric-

tions in his own country. To the most farseeing it fore-
shadowed an end to Japan's exclusion. Each of the three
steamers had a sailing ship in tow. In complete disregard of
challenging guard boats, all moved swiftly to join the supply
ship which had already reached the American anchorage in
Yedo Bay.

Scarcely had the squadron settled in formation when it
was visited at a respectful distance by small boats bearing
artists. Their rapid brush sketches of the panorama were
soon selling like hot chestnuts in Yedo streets. In a land
without newspapers, word of the new arrival spread, the
inevitable grapevine adding such details as could be imagined. What went on between the Bakufu and the Americans was completely unknown to watchers on the shore,
but boats putting out with official delegations soon indicated that meetings were in progress on the ships.

Perry immediately refused to accept Uraga as the site
for the conferences, in spite of the fact that preparations had
already been completed there at the order of the "Emperor." The commodore had not forgotten the previous
Japanese emphasis on Nagasaki as the only port at which
contact with foreigners was allowed. He had won his point
then by refusing to deliver the President's letter at a city
notorious for its ignominious treatment of Dutch traders;
now he was determined to conduct negotiations nearer the
capital at a place affording better protection for his ships.
Meanwhile, surveying of the harbor against a Japanese
restraining order began.

Mention by the Japanese of an alternate conference site
at Kamakura finally indicated that they might compromise,
and eleven days after his arrival, Perry ordered the squadron in motion toward Yedo. As soon thereafter as the
Shogun's capital could be informed and a hard-riding

messenger return, an order was issued: *If the Americans land at Yedo, it will be a national disgrace. Stop them and have the meetings at Kanagawa.* The deadlock was ended. The Bakufu had sensed rising opposition to its conciliatory attitude toward the Americans, and so had agreed on this face-saving measure. Yedo remained inviolate.

The treaty house was brought piece by piece from distant Uraga and set up on a level plain just outside the small fishing village of Yokohama.* Perry in the meantime moved his ships to a new position opposite Kanagawa, where the Japanese commissioners had taken up their abode.

During the morning of the day agreed on for the opening of negotiations, the Japanese commissioners sailed in a gaily decorated barge from the neighboring town of Kanagawa, while hundreds of native craft were anchored close at hand. On board this assortment of boats and along the shore, the Japanese knelt with bowed heads as their dignitaries stepped ashore. Apparently planned to match the American landing in impressive formality, this Japanese prelude exceeded it in barbaric splendor.

Perry engineered his own appearance with the ceremony due his naval rank and an accredited representative of the United States. Some five hundred officers and men under Commander Buchanan's direction embarked in twenty-odd boats and approached the shore in formation. The men, equally divided between marines and seamen and armed with muskets and pistols, formed a lane through which the commodore would pass on his way to the treaty house. Officers were grouped at the newly constructed landing to receive him.

At a signal, Perry entered a white barge to the accompani-

---

* Although on record as the Kanagawa Treaty, the negotiations took place at this adjacent village.

ment of a minister's salute of seventeen guns from the *Macedonian*. This was the first sight of the commodore that the Japanese had had since his return, because, continuing the technique of the year before, he had remained behind the scenes as "Lord of the Forbidden Interior," and conducted all business through his officers. The force and elegance of his appearance in the splendor of full-dress uniform, with its gleaming stripes, epaulettes and buttons, were electrifying. The broad pennant with a gilt battle-ax at the top of its staff added to the effect.

Two huge Negroes led the procession, carrying American flags. Bands played martial music as Perry and his officers marched impressively to the treaty house. A salute of twenty-one guns was fired from the ships in honor of the Emperor, followed by seventeen guns for Hayashi, the chief commissioner, and the Japanese flag was hoisted to the masthead of the *Powhatan*. These honors pleased the Japanese, who appeared to understand the gesture.

Refreshments followed the formal exchange of credentials. The tiny bowls of their host's pipes, which necessitated refilling after two of three short puffs, did not long interest the Americans, and they were glad to get down to serious business. For this a smaller conference room had been prepared. Perry entered it with his son and secretary, Lieutenant Oliver Perry; Captain Adams, and interpreters Dr. S. Wells Williams and A. L. A. Portman. The Reverend Mr. Williams, a well-known American Board missionary who had joined the squadron in China, was fluent in Chinese and had picked up a scanty colloquial vocabulary from Japanese fishermen who had been shipwrecked and stranded in China. Portman was well versed in Dutch. In the outer hall, Prime Minister Abe remained unidentified throughout the proceedings while Manjiro, the only Japanese in the empire with firsthand knowledge of the Americans, was some sixteen miles away behind fortified gates.* The opening formalities within the conference room were painful to the Americans. No sooner were they seated than they beheld the Japanese interpreter prostrate at the feet of Hayashi. Then he rose to his knees and dragged himself between his superior and the commodore with whispered felicitations, his gaze directed to the floor.

The answer to the President's letter was presented to Perry in the form of a long scroll. The Japanese acceded to the demands for better treatment of shipwrecked sailors and for supplies to needy ships. They offered one trading port and said that five years would be needed to complete arrangements, though restricted traffic could begin shortly. Apparently as a ruse which would nullify the agreement—this had been the tactic employed in dealing with Commodore Biddle who had headed the first American naval expedition to Japan eight years before—the commissioners had

---

* The completely erroneous statement that Manjiro was concealed in the treaty house during the negotiations appears to have first been made by the historian, William E. Griffis, in his *Matthew Calbraith Perry*, a biography published in Boston in 1887.

When Manjiro visited his benefactor, the Reverend S. C. Damon, in Honolulu in 1860—ten years after their parting—he reviewed his experiences, modestly saying in response to questioning: "I have been very often consulted respecting questions relating to Americans and foreigners. . . . I was in Yedo for a period of Commodore Perry's visit, but was not introduced to any of the officers of the expedition." (*The Friend,* June 1860)

Griffis misquoted *The Friend* in the following words: "Unknown to any of the Americans, Nakahama Manjiro who had received a good common school education in the United States, *sat in an adjoining room, unseen but active, as the American interpreter for the Japanese. All the documents in English and Chinese were submitted to him for correction and approval.*" (Italics are supplied by this writer.)

This reference was picked up by Frederick Wells Williams, then preparing a biography of his father, *The Life and Letters of Samuel Wells Williams LL.D.* (G. P. Putnam & Sons, 1889) and given wide

not signed the document. The alert Perry discovered the omission in time to leave the document in the treaty house with the request that it be attested and delivered to him aboard ship the following day.

A side conference between the commodore and Hayashi presented an opportunity to bring up the subject of the hoped-for treaty, but Perry was content not to press it. As part of his seed sowing he presented a printed copy of the commercial treaty which had been made between the United States and China when trade between those countries had been established. He stated that he had brought it along with the hope that it would be read; if Japan decided to grant commercial privileges to the United States, it might prove a helpful guide. With it he presented a rough draft of a treaty on which he had worked with Williams, and which he hoped to complete with Japan's

---

credence since the elder Williams was Perry's official interpreter with the expedition.

In 1891 when Dr. Inazo Nitobe wrote *The Intercourse Between the United States and Japan,* one of a series of Johns Hopkins University studies in Historical and Political Science, Manjiro was still living, but was apparently not consulted, for the error was not rectified.

Still later (1905) John S. Sewall, who, like Williams, had been with Perry, repeated Griffis' statement with embellishments of his own. In his book, *The Log of the Captain's Clerk* (privately printed, Bangor, Me.), Sewall made use of Manjiro's report to Mr. Damon, using full quotes as follows: " 'Where were you at the time of the expedition?' asked the chaplain. 'I was in a room adjoining that in which the negotiations were going on,' said Nakahama. 'I was not allowed to see or communicate with any of the Americans. But each document from Commodore Perry I translated before it was handed to the commissioners and the replies I also translated into English before they went to the commodore.' Which explains," adds Sewall, "what so mystified our diplomats at the time that the papers from 'the party of the second part' came to them not alone in Dutch but in English also."

The most widely quoted Japanese writer on the subject of Manjiro is Ishii Kendo, whose *Ikoku Hyoryu Kidanshu* was published in

assistance. When he left the treaty house, Perry felt that negotiations had opened auspiciously.

Sessions in succeeding weeks were tedious and time-consuming, owing largely to the lack of an interpreter with sufficient English vocabulary and background, the equivocation of the Japanese and their insistence upon Dutch as a third medium.* The Japanese opposed every point and wasted days over hairsplitting provisions.

Yet the patience and gentlemanly conduct of the harassed commissioners were at all times remarkable. Wrote Samuel Wells in retrospect:

> It is fair to give the Japanese officers the credit of showing none of that hauteur and supercilious conduct which the perusal of books about their country might lead one to suspect. Compared with

Tokyo in 1927. However, his is a narrative of several Japanese who were shipwrecked during Japan's isolation and drifted to foreign countries. His information on Manjiro, the most important of the group, is incomplete.

"The statement that Manjiro was in the treaty hall is all a myth," stated Manjiro's son, the late Dr. Toichiro Nakahama, to this writer. Dr. Nakahama was then at work on a biography of his father and had consulted every available source, including the family records of Manjiro's patron, Egawa Tarozaemon. Moreover, he said, translations done by Manjiro for the officials were in English only, since he had never studied either Chinese or Dutch, and his fluency in Japanese was newly acquired.

In his biography *Nakahama Manjiro den*, Dr. Nakahama states: "It is natural that many Japanese and Americans as well believe that Manjiro acted as interpreter at the conference since he was the only Japanese familiar with American people and customs at that time. However, he was not allowed to go to Kanagawa where the negotiations were held. But he did translate to the Japanese officials the American documents and acted as their adviser while living with Egawa in Yedo."

* Wrote Consul General Harris at a later date: "One would think the translation of a paper to be a simple process, but it is not so with the Japanese; for they are so absurd as to wish to have every word

the conduct of the Chinese when Amherst went to
Peking, that of Hayashi and his colleagues appears
far superior in point of courtesy, decorum and
willingness, as well as good sense in discussing the
matters brought forward for their acceptance.

Bit by bit the Treaty of Amity and Friendship was
molded. This provided, in the main, for humane treatment
of shipwrecked men, provisioning under certain conditions
of foreign ships, the use of two ports, and the residence in
Japan of an American consul general. It was almost more
than Perry had hoped for and he was immensely pleased. It
was the outcome of careful preparations on his part, begun
in 1852 when he had visited New Bedford and Fairhaven to
interview men who had survived atrocities in Japan and sea
captains who had picked up shipwrecked crews in the Pacific. By careful planning, showmanship and the power of
unused guns, he had broken down Japan's isolation. Almost
immediately, Great Britain, Russia and the Netherlands
were pressing for like treaties.

---

placed in the Dutch version exactly in the order it stands in the
Japanese. It is very difficult to explain to them the idioms of language, or the grammatical structure of it, or to get them to see that,
although the placing of the words does not correspond with theirs,
yet the meaning is the same. Their knowledge of Dutch is imperfect.
They have learned the language as spoken by traders and sailors, and
the Dutch they use is not only that of two hundred and fifty years
ago, but it is limited to the subjects above referred to; hence we have
great difficulty in conveying an abstract idea to them, and it is
almost impossible to speak figuratively to them."

22

Honors and Life Off Stage

WORD OF Manjiro's experiences in the mysterious West had spread rapidly, and scholars and progressive samurai sought personal interviews. Such men were supplying the country with mental vigor, and Egawa was in sympathy with them. But encroachments on his assistant's time were becoming serious, for he was required at all times to serve the needs of the Bakufu. Such business must take precedence over everything else.

A request from the Astronomical Bureau for his services was also of secondary importance, Egawa felt. Please, he wrote the Bakufu, do not take Manjiro from me. I need him in fulfilling my obligation to the country in this time of urgent necessity. Also please allow the whaleboat and other belongings confiscated at Nagasaki to be sent to me here. We need many such boats, for they are seaworthy and swift.

Seemingly simplicity itself, this Western whaleboat was like nothing the Japanese had ever seen. Manjiro displayed it proudly. He remembered how Massachusetts whalemen regarded their boats. Long years of development had perfected these "cockleshells." They were sharp at both ends, "clean sided as a mackerel"; they measured about twenty-seven feet long with a six-foot beam, had a depth of twenty-two inches amidships and thirty-seven inches at the bow and stern. They could ride the heaviest sea and withstand the fiercest gale. A trial convinced the Japanese that their clumsy craft were outmoded. Under Egawa's direction, hundreds of the new whaleboats were built during the following months.

Egawa also requested that Manjiro's instruments of navigation be sent to him, together with his books. After long delay they arrived, and Manjiro discovered that his English grammar was missing. It was the most sought-after book in all Japan and had doubtless been laboriously copied by hand.

Living in the aristocratic section of the capital, Manjiro was, paradoxically, both a prisoner and a much-honored man. References to him in official correspondence in the year 1853 suddenly indicated that by special dispensation he was now Nakahama Manjiro.* The bestowal of the surname, derived from his ancestral village, immediately placed him in a unique position. To the man once proud to be called John Mung because it set him apart as an individual, it must have seemed like an incomprehensible dream. He had earned this distinction for his family, and future generations would carry the name. He was proud also of the new family *mon,* or crest, which consisted of three dots within a bold circle and was worn on the sleeves and at the front and back of each garment.

Egawa's wish to keep Manjiro as his permanent assistant brought a still greater honor. The Prime Minister had written Lord Yamanouchi at Kochi requesting that Manjiro be transferred to the Bakufu, and a letter expressing profound thanks for the high honor to the Tosa clan had

---

* This was the old form of writing the family name first. For consistency in this narrative the name remains simply Manjiro.

been received in return. News of the transfer was generally regarded with astonishment, for a samurai under the Bakufu was recognized as of higher rank than if he were a retainer of a clan daimyo. That he was often treated with the respect of a hatamoto was equally remarkable because that rank implied hereditary prestige. The advice of Mito Nariaki, "Treat generously while guarding carefully," had been followed to the letter!

But a shadow rested over Manjiro's happiness as he began to realize that he was never to meet the American commodore. Egawa was angry too at a trick which had been played on him. Supported by his retainers, Egawa had gone to the treaty house on schedule, only to learn that the deliberations had already been concluded, with Hayashi presiding, and the treaty was about to be signed. It was clear that the wrong date had been given him to prevent his having a voice in the proceedings. Because of his outspoken praise of Manjiro, and his desire to profit by Western inventions and boatbuilding skill, Egawa was now frequently classed as proforeign by radicals who opposed the opening of the country.

Manjiro left no clue to the distress he must have felt during the stay of the American squadron in Japan. The growing faction bitterly opposed to foreigners, led on by hotheads sworn to kill Perry on sight, was a constant worry. Such an act would disgrace Japan in the eyes of the world and bring on a terrible retaliation.

He surely knew too of Moriyama Yenosuki, then acting as official interpreter, who had been a pupil of the half-caste American Indian, Ranald MacDonald, during the latter's imprisonment at Nagasaki. In Honolulu Manjiro had learned the details of MacDonald's rescue with the *Lagoda* crewmen and was aware that he had received less severe treatment at the hands of the Japanese because of his services as an instructor in English. Beyond this, nothing was known at the time. Now the sudden appearance of one of MacDonald's pupils in the role he himself had hoped to fill could have seemed little short of tragic to the man who by education and experience in dealing with foreigners was better prepared.* His resentment toward the course events had taken was quite natural and was shared by his friend Egawa, who had been most shabbily treated.

With the favorable turn of negotiations, Perry had set out to provide sumptuous entertainment for the Japanese commissioners. The banquet and minstrel show on his flagship were the gossip of the capital. Never had anything so elaborate or amazing been conceived. Even the dignified Hayashi had unbent, while his colleagues were often convulsed with mirth at Negro songs and dialogue. Moriyama had been among the guests.

It is probable that this was but one of the choice bits of news filtering in to Manjiro, and that the already disgruntled Egawa discussed developments with him quite freely. A strong bond of friendship had been forged between the two and they shared the same progressive views with regard to opening the ports.

Concerning American presents to the "Emperor" there had been public discussion, though doubtless only the commissioners knew that Perry had made it clear that these tokens of friendship were not to be regarded in the same light as the tribute long exacted of Dutch traders. By forcing acceptance of the President's letter on his first visit, his

---

* While MacDonald's instruction had been elementary, his diary reveals that his answer to a question concerning the relative grades of those composing the American government had been: "First, the People, and second, the President." Thus from his prison "cage" the first American in Japan had stated a fundamental principle of democracy which the first Japanese ever to visit the United States had amplified during his own prison trials.

continued refusal to go to Nagasaki for negotiations and this clear expression of principle, the American commodore had cleverly gained a toehold for democracy.

Among the gifts were a quarter-sized locomotive, car and tender, several miles of track and electric telegraph instruments with connecting wires—the very things Manjiro had labored to explain! While the steamships concerning which he had been endlessly queried lay at anchor for all and sundry to see! Amusement at the operation of the railway as seen by officers of the squadron was hardly shared by Manjiro, politely detained elsewhere.

Stated the official Perry report:

> All parts of the mechanism were perfect, and the car was a most tasteful specimen of workmanship, but so small that it could hardly carry a child of six years of age. The Japanese, however, were not to be cheated out of a ride. . . . It was a spectacle not a little ludicrous to behold a dignified Mandarin whirling around the circular road at the rate of twenty miles an hour, with his loose robes flying in the wind. As he clung with a desperate hold to the edge of the roof, grinning with intense interest, and his huddled-up body shook convulsively with a kind of laughing timidity, while the car spun rapidly around the circle, you might have supposed that the movement, somehow or other, was dependent rather upon the enormous exertions of the uneasy Mandarin than upon the power of the little puffing locomotive which was so easily performing its work.

And the telegraph! A message sent from one end of the wire arrived at the other extreme before swift runners could cover the distance, and was plainly read in both Japanese and Dutch languages! Careful examinations of the wire revealed no inner speaking tube. Magic? What else?

Did Manjiro hear of brave Yoshida Shoin (Torajiro)*
who, informed of his returned countryman's opportunities
in the West, and seeking the same for the benefit of Japan,
had attempted to board one of Perry's ships under cover of
darkness?

And was he told of the far-less-heroic shipwrecked national dubbed "Sam Patch"† who, returning from China
with Perry, completely lost his nerve at sight of his restricted home shores and whimpered and groveled before
Japanese officials boarding the ships? In returning home
without the sustaining might of a foreign navy Manjiro was
by comparison a very brave man. Did he realize this and
was there a shred of comfort in the thought?

Or did he find satisfaction in the sudden magnanimous
gesture of the Bakufu which placed him in complete charge
of all the gifts brought by Perry? Only after the squadron
had sailed and there was no possibility of contact was he
free to assume his new duties and to discuss with Egawa
many details of mechanical construction in which he was
interested.

And Perry? Flushed with the success of his diplomatic
game of hide-and-seek and his treaty making, he left Japan
completely unaware of a mystery play on shore that exceeded his wildest imagination. Of the dual government of
Emperor (impotent hereditary ruler, safely out of reach)
and Shogun (military usurper, supreme as governing power
in Yedo for six centuries) he was completely unaware. And
of Manjiro, his off-stage ally, he was never to know.

---

* "Yoshida Torajiro," wrote Robert Louis Stevenson four decades
later, "is a name probably unknown to the English reader, but which
should become a household word like Garibaldi or John Brown." See
Appendixes for Perry's account of this episode and its tragic outcome.
† The story of Sam Patch appears in the Appendix.

23

In the Wake of Perry

WHEN the sloop-of-war *Saratoga* arrived in Honolulu harbor, the town was agog with anticipation. The crowds soon learned that a treaty with Japan had been signed and Captain H. A. Adams, as Perry's courier, was bearing copies in English, Dutch and Japanese to Washington with the request that they be ratified before other powers might interfere.

Editor Damon was among the first to board the ship and to *The Friend* went the distinction of being the first American newspaper to print the news. There then being no Pacific cable, it was not until the bearer of dispatches reached San Francisco that the waiting world was informed of the historic event.

Damon had had no word from Manjiro for almost four years, and he sought information concerning him from the ship's chaplain and other officers. None had heard of the American-educated youth and everyone was incredulous. None believed that he had survived the ordeal of homecoming.

Damon was interested in the fact that Japanese officials had known before Perry arrived of the course pursued by the United States in settling the Mexican war. They were surprised, he was told, that after the Americans conquered the country they had paid a large purchase price to the conquered people. This was not the usual course pursued by victors in battle!

Could the information concerning American policy have come from Manjiro? Damon wondered. It was certainly one of the matters they had discussed together. Without knowing whether or not he had escaped the death penalty, it was still an interesting idea.

The officers told a story of Japanese confusion on a point of American citizenship, which was recorded by Editor Damon and often discussed on the docks and at private dinner parties. On a monument erected over the grave of a Marine who had died and been buried on Japanese soil, the birthplace of the deceased was given as Ireland. The Japanese did not understand the explanation and were distressed at the clear implication. Under American laws, they were told, a child born in Japan of American parents would be rated an American. Perry, they well knew, had explosively rejected a proposed clause in the treaty forbidding residence of American women in Japan. Now might American citizens be born in Japan? they asked in effect.

Manjiro must have smiled ironically as he assumed the duties of curator of the American presents. But only to himself, for he was painfully learning that a samurai was a stoic by immutable tradition. Exhausted by long hours of translating and interpreting, he felt, indeed, a crushing sadness. It was more than three months too late for him to feel satisfaction from showing examples of American ingenuity and industry. Over and over he explained the uses of air pumps, electric machines, horseshoe magnets, compasses and barometers. The task became monotonous. To those without an interest in mechanics, the most fascinating exhibits seemed to be Audubon's beautifully illustrated *Birds of America* in three volumes and his *Quadrupeds*. They were indeed treasures to the beauty-loving people. Finally, the entire display was relegated to distant Shidzuoka where the last Shogun lived in retirement, to be discovered later by one of the first American teachers in Japan during his rambles.* The Emperor to whom they were addressed never saw them!

Happily he resumed his work with Egawa, with activities extending from boatbuilding to breadmaking. Early Christians had introduced in Japan a spongecake called *kasutera* (for Castile) which was rated a great delicacy, and a kind of bread called *pan* was known to a few. Manjiro's recipe, straight from a New England kitchen, delighted the versatile Egawa. He persevered through failure and became known as Japan's first breadmaker. Building an out-of-door oven proved mere child's play to him, for he was already at work on a reverberatory furnace—the first in Japan—which was to bring him fame. He also experimented with movable type, an innovation from China which was eventually to make Japan the most literate of Asian countries.

A home of his own was something Manjiro needed to make him completely happy, Egawa decided. At twenty-seven he was many years past the age at which most Japanese married. Acting as go-between, Egawa began arrangements for a suitable marriage. Manjiro doubtless had a voice in the proceedings since he had learned, among other freedoms, the choice of a life mate. The prescribed "mutual seeing" may have partaken of the nature of a brief courtship. However, in this center of feudalistic ceremony cus-

---

* E. Warren Clark, a college friend of Dr. William E. Griffis, the historian, who was called by him to teach at Shidzuoka, and who later joined him at the school which became the Imperial University of Tokyo. Manjiro had resigned from this school before the two Americans became members of the faculty in association with the famous Dr. G. Verbeck.

tom was not easily set aside, and lengthy correspondence by special messenger with Manjiro's mother and the headman of his village, as well as many consultations with the parents of the prospective bride, fell to the lot of Egawa. Information as to the young woman's character and disposition, and her education in the fine arts of flower arrangement and the serving of ceremonial tea was gathered through discreet sources. An exchange of gifts bound the betrothal.

O Tetsu, chosen for her beauty and vivaciousness in contrast to her more demure older sister, was a daughter of Danno Gennoshin, a famous fencing master of samurai class. She was seventeen and very lovely in the costumes prescribed for the lengthy ceremony.

White being the symbol of mourning, the bride was first arrayed in a kimono of pure white, signifying that she was dead to her own family and henceforth under the direction of her husband's parents.

The wedding banquet was held at the home of the groom. During its progress the bride's costumes were changed three times. They were of the finest silk, and each seemed more beautiful than the one preceding. Each *obi*, or sash, a specimen of the weaver's highest art, was tied at the back in a large butterfly bow. In its front folds was tucked a small mirror case. The bride carried a folded fan.

An essential part of the feast was the *sansan ku-do*, or "three three, nine times," in which both bride and groom sipped three times from each of three beautifully lacquered sake cups of graduated sizes, making nine times in all. The pledge repeated in an inner chamber in the presence of the go-between concluded the marriage ceremony.

Adorning the wall in the banquet room was a scroll depicting the gods Izanagi and Isanami, the first married couple in Japanese history. On a tray the symbolic pine, plum and bamboo were arranged. Bits of dried fish and seaweed, signifying the hardihood of the Japanese race, were attached to the gifts. Custom also decreed that three days after the marriage the bride pay a "return home" visit wearing a kimono given by her husband. Her registration was then changed to the government office in which her husband's family records were kept.

After the marriage, the relationship between Egawa and the young couple was doubly close. The new home established within their patron's compound became a happy one for Manjiro and his bride.

After this pleasant interruption, shipbuilding went forward with all speed, and within a year a two-masted ship was built at Uraga for the Bakufu. Manjiro was superintendent of construction. When orders already in hand were filled, there would be many ships, but what about the skill to sail them? Egawa took the lead in urging the study of Western nautical science and the Bakufu ordered Manjiro to translate his recently recovered Bowditch's *New American Practical Navigator.**

It was a monumental task to translate so technical a book. Japanese equivalents for needed terms often had to be invented, to become finally a permanent part of the language. Manjiro was given a corps of skilled calligraphers, but he alone was responsible to the government for the task. He needed much help, for he had never had advanced studies in written Japanese.

Twenty-two volume sets, containing diagrams and logarithmic tables, skillfully executed with brush and ink, were

---

* It has at times been erroneously stated in Japan that the navigation text translated by Manjiro was by E. C. Blaunta (or Branter). This apparently results from phonetic spelling. Edmund Blunt was the *publisher* of Bowditch's famous book and it was written at his request as the need for an easily understood work on navigation developed. To Captain Whitfield and Chaplain Damon, both familiar with Bowditch, there was no question that he was the author.

completed at the end of eighteen months. He once remarked that the work had aged him three years. A little
grimly he remembered the story told in Fairhaven that
Nathaniel Bowditch, the mathematical genius who wrote
the book, had begun to turn gray at the age of twenty-one.
Manjiro himself had many gray hairs by the time the work
was completed.

Becoming available at a time when a demand for Western
science was at fever heat, this work into which Manjiro put
heart and soul exerted a tremendous influence, greatly
accelerating ship construction throughout the empire. In
what became a rivalry, the Satsuma, Mito, and Tosa clans
were building new ships, none as yet equal to the new
demands.

24

Cruise of a Whaler

EVEN AS he rejoiced in the birth of his first child, a daughter named Suzu (Musical Bell), Manjiro was plunged into sorrow by the death of Egawa Tarozaemon. The little girl had been named by his patron and the association made her doubly dear.

Manjiro well knew that both his advancement and his very life were due to his friend. The antiforeign element, already in evidence when he arrived in Yedo, had grown in numbers, and guards had to be employed. Constant vigilance had stayed the sword of more than one would-be assassin. Now the foreign-trained Manjiro must be more concerned about his enemies, though the patronage of the Egawa family was continued by the elder son. Within a few months he, too, was dead, and the second son succeeded to the name and position. He also felt an inherited responsibility toward his father's protégé.

A naval training school had been established in Yedo by the Bakufu and now Manjiro was installed as a member of the faculty. This was the school which Joseph Hardy Neesima, now known as the founder of Doshisha University, later attended to study mathematics. He recalled in his memoirs that it was the only school in the country offering such a course.*

After another year, the strain of grief and overwork began to undermine Manjiro's health, and he applied to the Bakufu for permission to visit his mother in Tosa. She was now past her sixty-first birthday. This auspicious occasion marked the completion of one cycle of the ten calendar signs and of the twelve zodiacal signs of the lunar calendar. On entering this new phase of life, a celebrant customarily wore a bright red piece of clothing, and made a visit to a shrine to express thanks for having been granted the privilege of attaining such a distinguished age. A home celebration followed. The celebration had been delayed, for the guest his mother most desired was her famous son, and he could not be immediately relieved of his responsibilities in Yedo. Now he felt he must go to Tosa, for the next important birth date would not occur until his mother became seventy, known as "the rarely reached age." Should she live to become seventy-seven, she would enter the "year of gladness" but that could not be foreseen.

Manjiro looked forward to the return trip over the Tokaido, for now sure happiness waited at the end of the road. He was treated with deference at the fifty-three post stations, for his costume and manner of speech were unmistakably those of a ranking official of the Shogunate. Yet he found glimpses of peasant life as entertaining as in that now seemingly far-distant time when it had been whispered along the road that he was one of the people controlled by a god of fortune.

---

* Neesima also remembered that when he made up his mind to go to America, in company with a sympathetic sea captain, he wrote his father a farewell letter. This was not delivered lest the friend to whom it was committed, and the father also, be subjected to severe punishment by the government, and three years elapsed before the father heard from his son.

From Kyoto to Osaka the returning son traveled by small ship; a larger ship conveyed him to the Kochi port.

It was a particularly happy time for both Manjiro and his mother.

Not long after Manjiro's return from Tosa to Yedo, Lord Abe, the Premier, died. This great man had shown extraordinary kindness to Manjiro in the days when the outcome of Perry's demands lay in the balance and Manjiro had been consulted because of his knowledge of the American people. Now Manjiro could better understand the great gulf that the Prime Minister had had to bridge in the emergency. Bred to the dignity and exclusiveness of high office, Lord Abe had unhesitatingly expressed confidence in Manjiro's integrity, and his inquiring mind had not been slow to catch the vision of a world in which Japan must play her part. The Premier had been criticized by many for failing to drive out the foreigners, but Manjiro—along with his friend and patron Egawa—had loyally supported the Prime Minister as a wise statesman.*

Manjiro had met Kawaji Toshiakira, the Minister of Finance, when he first came to Yedo. Now he outlined a plan to Kawaji to begin a government whaling project. The idea was at once accepted as a means of bolstering the national economy and as a method of training crews in navigation. Kawaji wished to begin at Hakodate, the newly opened port on the northern island of Hokkaido. Western whaling ships had found adjacent waters teeming with whales. Manjiro was sent to take charge of operations under

---

* Townsend Harris wrote of Lord Abe: "I am sorry to hear of the death of Abe Ise-no-Kami at Yedo. He was the second member of the Council of State and very influential. He was always represented to me as a man of great intelligence, and one that fully understood the power of the United States and other Western nations, and above all, was convinced that the time had arrived when Japan must abandon her exclusive policy, or be plunged into the miseries of war. He is a great loss to the liberal party of Japan."

the general direction of the governor. He was also to consider agricultural developments for the new frontier, and especially to make an experiment with Perry's Irish potatoes. Disclaiming an expert knowledge, Manjiro was yet familiar with rotation of crops as practiced in the United States; he had read in *The Friend* that potatoes were more valuable than rice as a preventive of scurvy, and he was glad to hear of the contemplated large-scale production.

Manjiro had seen many strange people on his voyage around the world; none were stranger than the Ainu who lived in this northern region. They seemed a race apart, living within Japanese territory but not Japanese. Their long hair and beards were strange, and their worship of the bear placed them apart. They paid little or no attention to agriculture. As with the American Indians, new developments had pushed them back into more limited territory instead of embracing or benefiting them.

A year and a half later Manjiro had completed his mission and was back in Yedo. Russia had presented a schooner to the Bakufu, which immediately called upon Manjiro to convert it into a whaler. Crow's nests were attached to the masts, whaleboats were built and installed and the hull was painted black. It was Japan's first "black ship."

But it did not live up to expectations. Manjiro sailed as captain on a whaling cruise in the direction of the Bonin Islands and ran into a storm of typhoon proportions. The ship was almost given up for lost, but Manjiro saved her by cutting down one of the masts. He wished to continue whaling, but an order from the Bakufu interrupted the new enterprise.

Townsend Harris, the first consul general from the United States, had arrived in Japan some three years before. He was at first unwelcome, and without naval power to sustain him, he had found progress difficult. By patience and good will he had finally won the confidence of the Bakufu, and under extraordinary circumstances had been allowed to visit the Shogun in person, a privilege not vouchsafed Perry. Now Harris had secured the agreement of the Tokyo government to commercial treaties with the United States. The next step was ratification at the national capital. Harris had encouraged a personal visit to Washington by Japanese ambassadors. The United States Government offered the steam frigate *Powhatan* for this important journey. As a countercourtesy the Bakufu proposed an escort ship, the *Kanrin Maru,* a three-hundred-ton sailing ship recently purchased from the Dutch. An auxiliary steam engine was useful only for maneuvering in and out of harbors.

To make this trip Manjiro was granted leave of absence from the naval training school. Before sailing he called with other members of the party at the American Consulate and there met Hikozo Hamada, self-styled Joseph Heco, who was acting interpreter for the Consul General. Shipwrecked some time after Manjiro, Heco had been taken to San Francisco, and there had come to know W. M. Gwin, then of the United States Immigration Service, later a senator from California. With Gwin's help he had been educated in Baltimore, had called at the White House and had received papers entitling him to American citizenship. Their benefactors, Gwin and Samuel C. Damon, were friends, but Manjiro and Heco seem not to have had more than a passing acquaintance, due perhaps to their difference in temperament. Heco was an opportunist while Manjiro voluntarily remained in the background. In 1862 Heco, temporarily in Hawaii, was suggested by Foreign Minister Robert C. Wyllie, for the position of Hawaiian Consul to Japan. King Kamehameha IV rejected the proposal on several grounds: Hawaii had no treaty with Japan; a recently received circular issued at the order of the Shogun, and forwarded by Consul General Harris, stated explicitly that it was the present policy not to make treaties other than those already concluded with foreign powers.

25

Prowess as a Navigator

SINCE the opening of the ports many students had concentrated on the study of navigation. By 1860 skilled navigators were believed available, and the Bakufu could complete the plans to send an escort ship with the *Powhatan*. It was a matter of pride that only seven years after their first sight of a steamship, the Japanese had become competent enough to sail their own ships. Manjiro was chosen to accompany the delegation as instructor in English and foreign ways. He had recently completed a small book on conversational English, including such phrases as "Good day, sir" and "How do you do, sir?" with their equivalents in Japanese. It was now part of his teaching equipment.

Ranking officer on the *Kanrin Maru* was Kimura, lord of Settsu, and Katsu Rintaru (Katsu Awa) was named captain. Katsu was a rising young Tokugawa retainer who had made phenomenal progress under Dutch teachers at Nagasaki. Seven years before he had stood admiringly on a bluff when Perry's squadron had first appeared offshore. Later he had been among the troops stationed in the background during the delivery of the fateful letter from the American President. Now he looked eagerly forward to a close observation of the Western world.

With all his enthusiasm, Captain Katsu was unable to

181

overcome the seasickness that drove him to his cabin before the *Kanrin Maru* had been long in the open sea. He was in a dilemma, for the honor of Japan was at stake. On board by courtesy of the Bakufu was Captain John Brooke, whose ship, the U.S.S. *Fenimore Cooper,* had been wrecked while taking soundings in waters near Japan. Captain Katsu had resented the fact that the well-known American captain would sail on his ship. It seemed to cast a reflection on his ability as a navigator. Very earnestly he wished to prove to the world that Japanese navigators needed no assistance in sailing their ships. But a storm of typhoon strength* and exhaustion from his illness forced him to order Manjiro to take command.

So great was the fury of the sea that the *Powhatan* suffered damage almost immediately and changed her course toward Honolulu to seek repairs. "The worst storm ever encountered in the Pacific" was the unanimous verdict of seasoned United States officers.

The sturdy little *Kanrin Maru* continued on to the California coast as planned, though for many days all its passengers could see from deep troughs in the sea was a deep wall of water. A merchant ship was once sighted; otherwise there were no sails. They were in a world of desolation and, to many, of terror.

At San Francisco, a correspondent telegraphed *Harper's Weekly* of the arrival of the ambassadorial escort ship "after thirty-seven days passage, Nakahama attending." Had Captain Whitfield recognized the name he would have appreciated, more than anyone else on either side of the Pacific, the significance of this brief item of news. His foster son was the

---

* The storm took a frightful toll in Japan where it was recalled by those opposed to the new treaties that Perry's first arrival had been marked by an uncanny meteor. Famine and many forms of pestilence increased the unrest.

first Japanese to navigate a ship across the Pacific, and he, Captain Whitfield, had been instrumental in giving him the knowledge to make it possible! It was now just ten years since the young prospector had left the Golden Gate determined to reach Japan, though uncertain of his fate at the hands of his countrymen. Surely, he too, must have been aware of the extraordinary success the years had brought.

Proudly, and for the first time in the life of the nation, the flag of the Rising Sun, flying from the masthead of the *Kanrin Maru,* was displayed in foreign waters. The new national emblem had been designed by Lord Shimadzu, of Satsuma. The Tokugawa family crest of three stylized leaves of the hollyhock with points meeting in the center—which had been prominently displayed during Perry's visit—was then believed by the Americans to be the national emblem.

The *Kanrin Maru* received a naval salute and a tumultuous welcome from the crowds gathered on the wharves. Badly in need of repairs, the ship was taken to the dry dock at Mare Island Naval Station. Those on board became guests of the city.

The mayor's and citizens' committees made elaborate plans for their entertainment, with Captain Brooke assisting in last-minute arrangements. The sight of dignitaries wearing long silk gowns with swords at their sides created a feeling of strangeness. But soon the greatest friendliness prevailed, though spoken words were necessarily few.

The eager and confident Manjiro was often dismayed and confused by the size of the town and by his failure to discover remembered landmarks. As the principal seaport for the thirty-first state, San Francisco had grown almost beyond recognition. There was now a railroad in the Sacramento Valley, he learned, the first in California, built four years before. Also San Francisco was linked with the Middle West by pony express.

Manjiro's success as a navigator had not increased his popularity aboard ship, though Captain Katsu had offered his personal expression of thanks. Official spies (politely listed as censors on the ship's manifest) watched intently for some untoward sign as he moved confidently about. Though he was a Bakufu official, his low birth was not forgotten, and his position as interpreter and adviser was often resented by men of jealous disposition. But as when he first returned to Japan, everyone found it expedient to rely on his firsthand knowledge of the Americans, and many asked him for guidance through the maze of strange streets.

At a reception for Lord Kimura and Captain Katsu at the International Hotel, Manjiro was in fine form, announcing each guest by name and official position. It was incomprehensible to the Japanese dignitaries that the governor of California and the mayor of San Francisco would arrive unattended by an impressive number of retainers. But assured by both Captain Brooke and Manjiro that this was evidence of American democracy, they accepted the situation and greeted their hosts with elaborate bows.

Among other courtesies extended to the visitors was a visit to a sugar refinery where the various processes were explained. Manjiro's companions were dumfounded at horse-pulled carriages, ice floating in glasses of water and champagne—ice, of all things, in warm weather!—and luxurious apartments with *private baths!* The sight of men and women dancing together in public hotels—the women with bare shoulders and hooped skirts—was almost too much for the visitors. Back in their hotel quarters they discussed the crude habits of the barbarians.

One of Manjiro's fellow passengers, Fukuzawa Yukichi, known later as "the father of education in Japan" and a foremost liberal, asked him to help in purchasing books to be used in the small progressive school Fukuzawa had founded in Yedo two years before. Both bought copies of Webster's *Dictionary;* Fukuzawa exulted in the fact that he had secured the most important book in the English language.* "Once I had secured this valuable work, I felt no hesitation in leaving the new world and returning home again," he said.

It is to be conjectured that Fukuzawa also took advantage of the rare opportunity to improve his English pronunciation in frequent conversations with Manjiro on board ship. In his autobiography Fukuzawa commented on the eagerly sought services of shipwrecked fishermen of a still later day:

> Occasionally there were shipwrecked Japanese fishermen who were brought back by foreign ships. These poor men had formerly, by government decree, not been permitted to re-enter this land, but after the new policy of "open ports" came into effect, they were allowed to return home. Whenever we heard of any such men, we called on them at their lodgings, and asked them to give us any English they knew.
>
> The pronunciation was naturally the most difficult part of all in the new language. The meaning and construction of a sentence was not so difficult. When, with the help of a dictionary, we replaced every word in the English sentence with a Dutch word, most of the sentences could be understood. So in studying the pronunciation, any child or uneducated fisherman who had been thrown with Englishmen or Americans could fill the place of teacher very well.

---

* For many years Fukuzawa's dictionary was on display at Keio University. An amazing recent discovery in a Tokyo secondhand bookstore was a copy of Manjiro's dictionary addressed on the title page to Hosokawa Junjiro, an intimate friend, who held important offices in the Meiji government, and became president of the Peers' School.

Among his personal purchases Manjiro most prized a daguerreotype apparatus with which to take his mother's picture. "And when that is done it will be useless." He also purchased a sewing machine, an invention he had never before seen, which, he felt, would be a treasured possession, little realizing that his mother, who all her life had sewn garments with long hand stitches, easily removed and replaced at each washing, would regard it without enthusiasm.

The *Powhatan* was eleven days late in reaching San Francisco, and paused only briefly to share in the city-wide entertainment. The embassy ship then proceeded to Panama, leaving the *Kanrin Maru* to return to Japan after completing repairs. The ambassadors reached the other side of the isthmus by train and continued on to Washington aboard the U.S.S. *Roanoke,* found waiting at Aspinwall. In the nation's capital they and their numerous attendants—a party of some ninety persons, including censors, physicians and barbers—were quartered in the fashionable Willard's Hotel where, a few months later, newly elected President Abraham Lincoln was to live with his family awaiting the inauguration. The ambassadors attended sessions of Congress, were received in state by President Buchanan, and were entertained at a White House ball and musicale.* Dr. Oliver Wendell Holmes honored the visitors with a characteristically effusive toast, and Walt Whitman wrote "A Broadway Pageant," which was to run through many editions of his *Leaves of Grass:*

---

* As at San Francisco, the visitors were amazed at the strange figures of American women. Reported *Harper's Weekly*: "One of the attendants on the ambassadors, a sharp little fellow [dubbed Tommy] . . . was at first a great pet of the ladies; but someone having persuaded him that hoops and their superstructure were 'solid' he made an attempt to verify the matter the other day, and since then the ladies are rather shy of him."

Over the Western sea hither from Niphon come,
Courteous, the swart-cheek'd two-sworded envoys,
Leaning back in their open barouches,
   bare-headed, impassive,
Ride to-day through Manhattan. . . .

26

"As One from the Dead"

LORD KIMURA, ranking officer of the *Kanrin Maru*, was especially observant on the voyage home. He had been instructed by his government to look out for uninhabited islands with a view to annexing them for Japan. Some of the officers on the ship wished to double Cape Horn and then sail around the Cape of Good Hope and through the Indian Ocean. Manjiro's accounts of his adventures had perhaps inspired such ambitious plans. But the size of their ship finally discouraged them and they decided to return, without further delay, by way of the Sandwich Islands.

Honolulu had given the ambassadors on the *Powhatan* an unprecedented show of hospitality. Minister of Foreign Affairs, Robert C. Wyllie, a Scotsman with an inherited regard for rank, had, by diligent inquiry, found that two of the visitors were princes of the highest rank. The final word came from the American Admiral Josiah Tatnall, who was in charge of the expedition. They were the first ambassadors ever to visit Honolulu, and it was fitting, and at the same time politically important, to offer every courtesy. Wyllie's own home, the famous "Rosebank," was too far up Nuuanu Valley to make it convenient for the visitors, so a house on Beretania Street, which he also owned, was quickly refurbished and offered in the name of the King.

This, he felt, would add a royal flourish to the occasion. Perhaps to ease his conscience, Wyllie wrote an explanatory note to the Reverend S. C. Damon, his pastor at the Bethel Church: "It really *is* the King's house because he acquired an unconditional surrender of it for the ambassadors and fitted it up magnificently for their reception on the day of their arrival."

Receptions and banquets had been lavish. At the Seamen's Bethel, Chaplain Damon had preached a sermon stressing the international significance of the embassy. Commenting on a map of Yedo, which the chaplain of the *Powhatan* had given him, Damon said wonderingly of the Japanese capital: "It is one big city, as large as seven fine towns in Berkshire County, and contains a population as large as the state of Massachusetts."

At what he considered an opportune moment, Wyllie queried the ambassadors on the possibility of a treaty of friendship and commerce between Hawaii and Japan similar to that in effect between the United States and Japan, but the visitors were not empowered to enter into any such agreement. He was disappointed, but the social brilliance of the visit remained undulled.

Having had a breathing spell, little Honolulu now proceeded to honor the newly arrived officials on the *Kanrin Maru*. The ship had brought the first mail from San Francisco in several weeks, and was thus doubly welcome. The whole population seemed to parade the streets.

A messenger from the King brought an invitation to Lord Kimura to visit the palace before noon. Manjiro was one of the attendants chosen to accompany him. He had seen the palace from the outside but had never before beheld the King. Now reigning, they learned, was Kamehameha IV, a name which sounded important since it indicated unbroken succession.

The visitors entered through an impressive iron gate in

the stone wall surrounding the palace, and faced a row of soldiers—sixty, Manjiro thought—whose officer saluted with his sword. At the palace steps they were received by the Minister of Foreign Affairs. With great ceremony he introduced them to the King. They soon retired and Captain Katsu was next received in audience.

At one reception the guests of honor were formally introduced to the venerable Governor Kekuanaoa, who was the last survivor of the royal party which had accompanied King Liholiho and his queen on their visit to England in 1823 to become acquainted with the ways of the world. It was reported that the governor looked sadly on these emissaries, fearing that they, like his lamented king and queen, would never return to their native land.

After gifts from the visitors were formally acknowledged, an invitation was extended to them to view the "national treasure." Since everyone on the ship was accorded this privilege during succeeding days, there was much speculation as to what this treasure might be. Among those greatly disappointed was Fukuzawa Yukichi, who recorded in his diary: "It was no more than a rug of innumerable feathers." Though undoubtedly a man of superior intellect, Fukuzawa was no judge of Polynesian art. What he had seen was the famous royal feather cloak, which a more appreciative writer of a later day described:

> The royal robe of Kamehameha I is a marvelous piece of work which rivals the arts of civilization. It is a large circular cloak (4½ x 7½ feet) almost four yards in circumference and made of tiny feathers. They are woven into an ingenious net work so that they lie as smooth as upon the neck of a bird—without a thread visible. The color is a brilliant yellow, the feathers extracted two at a time from living birds. These feathers were demanded as a tax by the king and chiefs. The robe

is said to have occupied successive reigns in its manufacture.

Fukuzawa was disappointed also in the ordinary European costumes worn by the King and Queen. A man, said to be the King's brother, was seen going to market with a basket on his arm. "So the King of Hawaii seemed to me more or less the head-man of a village of fishermen," Fukuzawa told in his diary.

The King, however, was exceedingly kind, sending large wooden bowls of fresh fish and fruit for all hands, and visiting the ship himself in company with the gracious Queen.

To Manjiro, Honolulu was filled with memories, and he longed for free time to explore once familiar parts of the town. With a full day at his disposal, he set out to find his friend Chaplain Damon. But new buildings and cross streets were confusing, and he finally had to inquire of a pleasant-faced little boy the direction of Chaplain Lane. "My home is there," said the boy. "I will take you." Then suddenly he asked, "Are you Manjiro? My brother told me about you." It was Eddie Damon, who had been only two years old when Manjiro had left Honolulu ten years before; he knew all about his brother Sam's hero. It could not then be conjectured that one future day the still younger boy, Frank, would be lavishly entertained in Japan, soon after the visit there of the Hawaiian King Kalakaua, in the same beautiful Maple Club and surrounded by Japanese gentlemen who had been recipients of the royal decoration. The pleasure of his Japanese experiences years later was to be sharpened by his family's deep interest in Manjiro.

The Damons welcomed Manjiro warmly. "We were never more surprised. He appeared as one from the dead," Damon told his newspaper audience. His costume, his rank, his story—all astonished the chaplain and his wife.

From the scabbard at his side Manjiro drew a sword and presented it to his benefactor. He stated that it was centuries old, forged by a famous craftsman, but not beautiful like the ceremonial swords customarily worn for dress. To the Japanese it had a meaning which was hard to explain. It was part of himself—his soul—which he humbly offered to his friend.

Then, with a happy smile, he took from his robe a package wrapped in silk, the four corners tied in the center. Damon turned the mysterious parcel in his hands, then delightedly drew forth two handwritten volumes with oriental characters reading from top to bottom of the pages and many familiar tables. It was Manjiro's translation of Bowditch's *New American Practical Navigator.** All the exacting work, all the fatiguing hours when he had squatted on his heels or lain awake at night trying to clarify difficult terms, were forgotten in his friend's warm praise.

From beginning to end it was a visit never forgotten. Manjiro's pride in his recently purchased gift for his mother was increased when he found Mrs. Damon using a new Wheeler and Wilson sewing machine which was an object of interest in Honolulu. Mrs. Damon explained that it had been ordered a year before and had come "round the Horn" in perfect condition.

The new three-storied Seamen's Home built three years before on land donated by the King surprised Manjiro. Dr. Judd had assisted the chaplain in collecting money from shipmasters and older residents. It was not far from where the old fort had stood; that landmark had been torn down three years previously.

Greatest surprise of all was the information that Captain Whitfield had seen the Seamen's Home dedicated and

---

* In 1876 exhibited by Mr. Damon at the Centennial Exposition in Philadelphia. This has since been lost.

had made a congratulatory address. With what joy did Manjiro hear of his old friend! The captain was now master of the *Gladiator,* and on another whaling cruise, he was told.

With a bound gift file of *The Friend* for the years 1852-1859,* Damon visited Manjiro on the ship and was introduced to Captain Katsu. It was a proud moment for Manjiro, representing as it did the American good will he had so many times talked about in Japan.

Ranking officers were guests that evening at a declamatory contest at Punahou School. The occasion was doubtless of special interest to Fukuzawa, who was to introduce public speaking in the schools of Japan. At first frowned on as a crude form of self-assertion, it was before long a popular course.

Four days after arrival the *Kanrin Maru* put to sea. A salute to the King and answering guns from Punchbowl echoed in the soft May air.

_____

* This personally inscribed volume is today a treasured possession of Manjiro's grandson.

27

Breakers Ahead

BEFORE leaving Honolulu, Manjiro wrote a letter to his old friend, Captain Whitfield. Two copies remain almost a century later—one in the possession of Whitfield descendants in Fairhaven and the other among Damon papers in Honolulu. Both are in Manjiro's handwriting, indicating, perhaps, that an attempt was made to improve the original.

They are an interesting psychological study. No longer are the diction and penmanship those of an honor student at Bartlett's Academy. There are misspellings, and the personal pronoun is often not capitalized. Had he forgotten the English forms in his struggle with Japanese idioms, or had he been influenced by the fact that the Japanese language possessed few pronouns, that personality was submerged through the use of terms signifying honor for the person addressed and self-abasement for the addresser? His reference to the Emperor seems to indicate that like many of his countrymen and the world in general, he was not aware of the divided sovereignty, and that power, not the individual, impressed him.

Even more interesting is Manjiro's confession of annoyance at Japanese spies. He does not call them spies, but he says: "I wish to send the letter from San Francisco *but so many Japanese eyes i can't.*" This to the one who "next to

God" is his best friend, is the only known record of complaint against the government by Manjiro. His letter reads:

SANDWICH ISLAND, MAY 2, 1860

CAPTAIN WILLIAM H. WHITFIELD.

My Honored friend—I am very happy to say that i had an opportunity to say to you a few lines. I am still living and hope you were the same blessing. i wish to meet you in this world once more. How happy we would be. Give my best respect to Mrs. and Miss Amelia Whitfield, i long to see them. Capt. you must not send your boys to the whaling business; you must send them to Japan, i will take care of him or them if you will. Let me know before send and I will make the arrangement for it.

Now I will let you know how am i arrived to my Native Country. You know that i have been to the Gold Mine; here stayed 4 month, average eight Dolls per day, beside expenses, from here i made my mind to get back and to see Dear Mother and also Shiped in one of the American Merchant men. In this vessel i arrived to Sandwhich Island. I found our friend Mr. Damon and through his kindness bought a whale boat and put her into a Merchantman. This vessel was going to Shanghai in China.

It was January very cold that part of country; Time i went on shore south off Great Loo Choo it was gail with snow. The Capt. of vessel he wish me to stay with him and to go to China, but i refused it, because i wanted to see Mother. The boat is ready for me to get in, myself, Dennovo & Goyesman jump into the boat, parted with ship at 4 P.M. After ten hours hard pull we arrived lee of Island and anchored untill morning. i went on shore amongst the Loo Choose, but i cannot understand their language, i have forgot all Japanese words. I stay here six months, under care of the King of Loo Choo, waiting for Japanese junk to come.

In the month of July get on board junk and went into the Harbour of Nagashirki Island, off Kie-u-see-u, waiting to get permition for 30 month before we get to our residence. After all the things is properly regulated we were send to our residence. It was great joy to Mother and all the relation. i have stay with my Mother only 3 day and night the Emperor called me to Jedo. Now i became one emperian officer. At this time i am attached this vessel.

This war steamer were send by Emperor of Japan to the Compliment of the President of America. We went to San Francisco, California, and now homeward bound, at Sandwich to touch Island to secure some coal and provition. I wish to send the letter from San Francisco but so many Japanese eyes i can't. i wrote this between passage from San Francisco to Island. Excuse me many mistakes. i can write better after our arrived Japan Jedo.

I wish for you to come to Japan. I will now lead my Dear Friend to my house, now the port open to all nations. I found our friend Samuel C. Damon. We was so happy each other I cannot write it all. When I get home I will write better acct. I will send to you sut of my clothe. It is not new, but only for remember me.

I remain your friend,

JOHN MUNGERO

As the Japanese ambassadors left Japan for the United States, the chauvinistic "Song of the Black Ships" had been on many lips:

> They came from the land of darkness,
> Giants with hooked nose like mountain imps;
> Giants with rough hair, loose and red;
> They stole a promise from our sacred master
> And danced with joy as they sailed away
> To the distant land of darkness.

On their return they found the chorus swelling to a crescendo. The assassination of the Premier Ii Kamon-no-kami had flamed to white heat antiforeign feeling. He had been attacked by Mito radicals as he approached the castle in Yedo, and his severed head hung on the main gate for all to see. The lesson was clear that no man, no matter how high in the Shogunate, could take irrevocable steps involving the country with foreigners.

Indignation centered around the treaty signed by Ii which the embassy had carried across the Pacific to have ratified; its members, pleased with their reception in the United States and favorably impressed by some of the democratic processes they had seen at work, could only make a a secret report to the Bakufu, leaving the country at large in ignorance of a new and cordial relationship.

For the first time in the long reign of the Tokugawa Shoguns there was opposition from the Kyoto court. What the end would be none could foresee.

Before many months H. C. J. Heusken, secretary to Consul General Harris, was struck down and killed as he rode near the American consulate. Soon all resident consuls, with the exception of the intrepid Harris, had fled Yedo. Regretting such incidents, and making every possible effort to protect the lives of high-placed persons of whatever nationality, the Bakufu found itself helpless.

To Manjiro sudden dismissal from the Naval Training School came as a sad anticlimax. Fresh from his success as navigator and warmed by the welcome given him at the Damon home in Honolulu, he had returned to Japan with new pride and self-confidence. He had been pleased with an invitation to visit an American ship which had arrived at Yokohama in the vanguard of trade. Then, with no opportunity to explain what to him was a perfectly natural and friendly act, he was accused of disclosing secrets to the Americans. The suspicion seems not to have originated with Ando, lord of Tsushima, who had been appointed Minister of Foreign Affairs, since he himself was attacked by antiforeign gangs. In the new disorder no explanation of individual disfavor seemed valid.

Then suddenly, with a complete change of face, the Bakufu sent Manjiro presents for meritorious service on the embassy escort ship! Lumps of gold and two suits of clothing were borne to him on lacquer trays by court messengers. This was the "honorable donation of the crested dress," one of the distinctions of feudal life. According to custom the honor of receiving the crested garments would be recorded in family history, dated and described as an event of hereditary importance. In the streets the common people prostrated themselves as the wearer passed. An empty tribute to a man who had done his utmost for his country and had now been deprived of his position in the important naval training school!

28

First English Letter

By 1861 the Bakufu had acquired territorial ambitions. Suddenly it saw a way to make use of Manjiro's ability to speak English without jeopardy of state secrets. Many officials remembered Commodore Perry's interest in the Bonin Islands as a supply station for Pacific whalemen and for ships in the China trade. They knew, too, that an American, Captain Coffin, had claimed discovery of them in 1823, and Captain Beechey, a Britisher, four years later. Nathaniel Savory's outspoken wish to gain a United States protectorate over the islands, and a junket to Honolulu by Matteo Mazarro seeking further aid from the British consul, had resulted in nothing but delayed action. It was apparent that the United States Congress did not look with favor on Perry's proposal, and that none of the great powers contemplated pressing a claim. Why shouldn't Japan take ownership by right of the earliest discovery of all? For in the sixteenth century a Japanese had ventured in that direction under orders from Hideyoshi, and in his honor the name, Ogasawara, had appeared on Japanese maps ever since. Now, the Bakufu felt, was the proper time to take possession.

The expeditionary force consisted of four ships. Manjiro

199

was assigned to the *Kanrin Maru,* the ship he had successfully navigated the previous year. He was the ideal man to
serve as interpreter, for he was familiar with the precarious
waters surrounding the Bonin and Volcano islands and was
personally acquainted with the foreign settlers.

They found that Matteo Mazarro had died and Nathaniel
Savory had taken over the governorship. He had married
Mazarro's widow, a native of Guam, who was to bear him
ten children.

The American flag was flying—it had been presented to
Savory by one of Perry's officers. But by now Savory cared
less about which flag flew than acquiring a stable constitu-
ency. He had had enough of devastated crops and prolonged
orgies by renegades from whaling fleets. When Japan's plans
for colonization were explained to him, he approved, saying
that anyone who would work was welcome. He wanted
especially land-loving families. Land was parceled out, lumber was unloaded from the ships and seemingly well-organ-
ized plans for settlement went forward. But when the ships
returned to their home base within a few weeks, only a few
clerks remained to enforce Japan's claim. Nathaniel Savory
did not live to see the formal annexation of the Bonins by
Japan in 1875, and Nakahama Manjiro had no part in that
territorial expansion.

In the distress occasioned by the loss of his naval position,
Manjiro was comforted by a letter from Captain Whitfield,
which was delivered by the Honorable Robert H. Pruyn,
minister-resident, who had succeeded Consul General Harris. Minister Pruyn had arrived in Japan April 25, 1862,
while the Bonin expedition was away. The letter was probably the first in English ever received by a Japanese. That
it was treasured its fine state of preservation in 1956 attests.
The letter reads:

SAN FRANCISCO
MAR. 9, 1862

TO THE FRIEND I HAVE NOT SEEN FOR A LONG TIME:

I have missed you for such a long time and now the newly appointed Minister offers to take a letter to you. If you care to send a reply after receiving this letter I hope you will take the same means which I am sure will bring your letter to me. I too will send more letters to you.

My wife is well and "Aunt" is married. My son Marcellus is thirteen years old now and grown to be as big as you were at the time of your sailing on the *Howland* years ago. I have two daughters, eleven and nine, both healthy and lovely.

The old gentleman next door still praises your honesty and good nature whenever he recalls the time you were at our home.

We are now trying to overcome a trouble in our country that may lead to serious consequences. War causes a great loss of life and wealth in any nation, but cannot always be avoided.

You must have become an important man by now. We are looking forward to the time we can trade with your country, and your people may come here and do business as ourselves. Why don't you come? Bring the Japanese products for sale.

Your sincere friend,
[Signed] WILLIAM WHITFIELD

Samuel C. Damon had given the new minister another commission. It seems logical to suppose that the incident referred to in the minister's report to Damon led to the delivery of Captain Whitfield's letter and that the stock of the disgraced Manjiro took a sudden upward bound with the Japanese Admiral witness to the episode. Minister Pruyn wrote:

> . . . On my arrival here I made inquiries about Manjiro, but could learn nothing of him. After

the arrival of the *Wyoming,* Commodore Mac-
Dougal made like ineffectual inquiries, till one
day we had a review of all the troops and saw the
Japanese Admiral, of whom the same inquiries
were made, accompanied by Commodore Mac-
Dougal's remark that he thought that he had recognized him in a crowd of spectators. He was
called forward. He had no swords and said that
he was in disgrace, and had not dared come forward until called. We did not learn the cause of his
disgrace.

The only valid explanation of Manjiro's appearance
without his swords appears to be that it was his own choice
at a time when he was unjustly reprimanded for going on
board a foreign ship. Nine years later the government was
to give permission to samurai to wear swords or not, as they
pleased. This was acknowledgment that the sword was no
longer considered an indispensable badge of gentility. The
custom was ultimately abolished by imperial edict.

Manjiro's newest purchase—the daguerreotype equipment—was also looked upon with suspicion if not alarm.
For the Japanese believed that when the likeness of a person was transferred to a photographic plate his soul departed. The reversal of the figure frightened them especially. Swords were never worn on the left side, and only
on a corpse did a kimono cross from right to left! It must
be more foreign magic.

Gradually natural curiosity overcame fear. No harm
seemed to come to the samurai who were brave enough to
sit for portraits. Crowds began to gather, and Manjiro found
himself engaged in a business he had not anticipated. To
his great satisfaction his wife had been the first to be photo-
graphed, and he would take his mother's picture on his
next visit to his ancestral village. It was amusing to find that
a new Japanese word, literally translated "copy truth," had
come into use with the daguerreotype.

The life of a photographer held no permanent charm for the owner of the improvised studio, and soon a friend took over the flourishing business.

In Yedo Manjiro had met one Hirano Renzo, a large landholder in Echigo province, who had come to learn about Western countries from the man who had actually visited them. He studied English and geography and was delighted that his teacher was able to explain the "flaming water" which issued from the ground and was rated one of the Seven Wonders of Echigo. The phenomenon had long puzzled the people of his province. On his recent trip Manjiro had heard of the discovery of petroleum in Pennsylvania, and this combustible "water" must, he felt, be the same substance. Manjiro showed him also how to preserve ice for summer use, a real benefit to the fishing industry.

Hirano it was who inspired Manjiro with the old whaling fever. Together they planned and financed a whaling cruise which began most auspiciously. After weathering a storm which drove them in the direction of the Bonin Islands, Captain Manjiro decided to make port for the purpose of building needed whaleboats. They had taken two sperm whales and prospects seemed bright.

None of the crew was capable of giving Manjiro the help he needed, but he believed he would find experienced boatbuilders among old settlers in the Bonins. He had brought along the needed lumber, and soon two whaleboats were taking shape on shore.

Among his hired helpers was one William Smith, a Britisher, who proceeded to pawn some of his possessions to the Japanese on the ship and then attempted to recover them by intimidation. Both he and his accomplice were armed. When the desperate character of the men was revealed, Captain Manjiro decided on prompt action. The men were handcuffed and written confessions were obtained at Port Lloyd in the presence of witnesses.

Testimonials concerning bad conduct in the past further incriminated the men.

At Yedo they were turned over to the British consul. Their trial is said to have been the first under the new treaties in which foreign criminals were under the jurisdiction of their own consular courts. This procedure seemed simple enough; it was some time later that extraterritoriality became a sore which festered in Japan's side.

Late in 1862 Manjiro's wife, who had been happily expecting their third child, fell ill and died, a victim to the severe epidemic of measles sweeping the land. The sorrowing Manjiro was thus harshly reminded of his country's need for improved sanitation and medical skill and immediately decided to have his eldest son trained as a doctor.

The child had been given the lucky name Toichiro ("First East Boy"), and great things were expected of him.

Manjiro felt a special pride in Toichiro on the fifth of each May. On that day huge paper carp flew from a long pole which projected from the roof of the family home, symbolizing, according to ancient tradition, determination to overcome difficulties. Like a carp fighting its way upstream, the growing boy would, it was believed, gain the strength to fight life's battles.

29

A World Upside Down

A NEW spirit of lawlessness had taken possession of the land. Bands of unattached samurai called "ronin" had long roamed the countryside, and now their numbers were growing rapidly. They were often actuated by a spirit of revenge and were feared, yet some of their exploits held romantic interest. The story of the Forty-seven Ronin, who after long waiting and self-denial had cut down the slayer of their master before taking their own lives, had become popular tradition.

The ronin felt increasing fury against the weakness of the Bakufu in admitting foreigners. They identified themselves as the "Barbarian-Expelling party," and sent forth their rallying cry, "Revere the Emperor, expel the Barbarians!" with shuddering effect. Trained to expert use of the sword, they were able to foment serious trouble. The powerless Bakufu could only issue warnings and advise foreigners not to go unarmed. Depredations continued. Men caught not in unlawful acts but accused only of "evil thoughts" were often victims.

Opinion varied regarding the best method of dealing with the foreigners. Simpler minds still hoped for the intervention of the Divine Wind—a typhoon—which had saved the country in the thirteenth century by driving away the forces of the invading Mogul emperor, Kublai Khan. Soon after Perry's arrival, in fact, an imperial edict had ordered prayers for a return of this saving power, but the squadron had departed safely. Other ships demanding trade were a continuing problem.

Extremists wanted to make a show of force, while the more realistic favored compromise with the foreigners. To yield until such time as adequate defenses could be built seemed to them the only wise course.

Personal attacks and the burning of legations continued and led finally to the "Richardson Affair," which was to bring serious reprisals. An Englishman named Richardson was riding on the Tokaido with three companions when they met an elaborate procession. The head of the Satsuma clan was returning home after a stormy session with the Shogun in Yedo. Because the foreigners failed to dismount and give immediate right of way as Japanese custom demanded, Richardson was slain on the spot; in the following confusion, his companions escaped. A public apology from the Bakufu further infuriated its enemies.

British authorities immediately demanded the apprehension and punishment of the offending clansmen. A year later, when these demands remained unsatisfied, British men-of-war appeared in Kagoshima Bay. An intensive, short-range siege, in the midst of a typhoon, laid the Satsuma capital in waste.

A sudden and unprecedented order from the Emperor's court confused the situation even more, for it summoned the Shogun to Kyoto to explain his weak policy toward foreigners. Amazingly, he complied, tacit acknowledgment of his weakening power. The imperial court set a date for the forcible expulsion of the foreigners, and ordered the Shogun to enforce the new edict—thereby undoing his own work.

On the day set, the province of Choshu began hostilities by firing on an American vessel anchored at the entrance to the narrow strait of Shimonoseki. An attack on French and Dutch ships followed. An allied counterattack subsequently destroyed many Choshu forts, and enormous indemnities were demanded.

Two of the strongest and proudest clans had now been humbled. First the threat of Perry's guns, then an object lesson in advanced warfare, had taught them that they urgently needed to learn the secrets of Western military power.

In the spring of 1864 the Satsuma clan, with new vigor and with unconcealed admiration for the power and skill of foreigners, opened a college called Kaisei-jo to train cadets along Western lines. The famous Nariakira, lord of Satsuma, the first to question Manjiro on his return to Japan, had died some time before, but his brother, Shimadzu Hisamitsu—acting for his son who had been named successor but was not yet of age—was effectively carrying forward educational projects and the manufacture of a new type of military equipment. Now more than ever there was need for concerted effort. As a center of rich iron and mineral mines, Satsuma was in a position to lead.

Shimadzu recalled Manjiro's familiarity with Western ships and dispatched a letter to the Bakufu requesting his services for a three-year period. Manjiro welcomed the assignment, for the death of his wife had left him desolate and no man's life was safe in the seething capital.

Accompanied by Tachibana—a classical scholar and his student follower—together with a servant, Manjiro set out. At Kyoto he met a resident retainer of Yamanouchi, lord of Tosa, who speeded his clansman on his way with a letter of praise to an official in Satsuma:

Manjiro is a navigation expert, and is familiar with foreign countries. He will be valuable in training a navy that will eventually tour the world. Cruises as far as the Ryukyus will be a good beginning.

At the Satsuma capital Manjiro entered at once into the operation of the naval training school. He alternately taught classes on land and conducted short training cruises at sea. He enjoyed wide contacts with officials of various clans whose quickened sense of a national emergency often brought them to him for advice. From this small beginning the powerful Japanese navy of the twentieth century was to emerge.

Certain Satsuma officials had been commissioned to buy ships, and Manjiro went with them to Nagasaki to assist in the purchase of five up-to-date steamers. Unfortunately, Japan was becoming a market for obsolete ships flying the flags of many countries. Daimyo who knew nothing of either the worth or operation of Western ships recalled the immense profits made by their ancestors in the early days of Portuguese trade and, undeterred by their lack of experience, bought recklessly. Foreign shipmasters took advantage of the ignorance of those to whom they sold and charged exorbitant rates of interest. Again Manjiro could be of real service.

It was unthinkable to Manjiro that he should be for any length of time in the vicinity of his home island of Shikoku without seeing his mother. He procured official leave and with Tachibana proceeded to Nakanohama. There was no lack of money now, and Manjiro immediately employed carpenters to build a new and more comfortable family home. A tile roof set it apart from other dwellings in the village, and more and larger rooms accommodated friends who called to pay their respects to Tosa's distinguished son.

Tachibana wrote a memorial in classical Chinese which extolled his teacher's filial loyalty and service to his country. The text ran:

... Manjiro has unusual virtue, as well as wealth and fame. Throughout the country everyone knows his name, from the Imperial Court down to the peasantry. He has made friends with most of the scholars of his time. He is most useful to the country. ...

The proud mother hung the hand-lettered scroll in the *tokonoma* of the new home. Earth for her could hold no higher joy.

By order of Lord Yamanouchi, Manjiro visited the capital to advise in the operation of the school which was then under construction as the outgrowth of the little English school he had organized soon after his return to Tosa from the Nagasaki trials. When completed it would contain a memorial tablet bearing Manjiro's name. In Kochi he met his early pupil, Goto Shojiro, who had become one of the leading men of the clan and was in charge of the construction of the new school. He would go far in helping his country meet new conditions.

Goto accompanied Manjiro to Nagasaki. They found no satisfactory ships there and went on to Shanghai, where they purchased one ship and supervised the building of another. When they returned to Nagasaki, they were amused to find at their hotel—grandiloquently called The Astor House—a team of Japanese acrobats which had been booked by an enterprising Englishman for an engagement in London. Always on the alert for something new, Manjiro purchased a music box from an English trader. Everywhere he could see indications of expanding trade.

30

The Fall of the Shogunate

ON THE expiration of his teaching contract in Satsuma, Manjiro returned to Yedo for a visit with his children. Living in the Satsuma headquarters at the capital, and with time to indulge the young samurai who came to him for information on many subjects, he devoted himself to an informal dissemination of Western knowledge. Gatherings had to be held without public notice, for the secret police were ever vigilant.

One terrible night, always remembered by eleven-year-old Toichiro, some five hundred enraged Bakufu soldiers and ronin attacked the clan headquarters and burned it to the ground. The open rebellion lasted only a few hours, but it left many casualties and is known as "the riot of 1867."

Two sudden deaths and a quick succession of events changed history. The Shogun died and his successor was Tokugawa Keiki, son of the retired lord of Mito. Keiki's rule was short. Difficulties on every side finally made his position untenable, and with his resignation went an acknowledgment that only by unity of thought and effort could the country hold its own with the nations of the world.

Opposition against the defeated cause continued for some time with sporadic fighting, but the power of the Tokugawa Shoguns was forever broken.

The Emperor Komai had died in Kyoto only six months after the death of the distraught Shogun whom he had called to account for the continued presence of the foreigners. The boy of fifteen who assumed his father's role was to be referred to years later with veneration as Meiji Tenno; but at that time the new Emperor was completely dependent on the advice of councilors who were also inexperienced but who were rapidly gaining wisdom in the heat of national upheaval. Strangely, these advisers were not the daimyo, who were great in name and wealth only, but young samurai who had caught some of the new vision and were pooling their advanced ideas to create a new order in government. Although never a politician, Manjiro could rejoice in the bold steps leading to reconstruction. These younger men, remaining largely in the background, were the force behind the changes taking place with almost breathtaking speed.

January 1, 1868, saw the opening of the new era for which the name Meiji—enlightenment—was chosen. The cry, "Expel the barbarians," was no longer needed as a political tool for the embarrassment of the Shogun and had lost its force. And the die was cast when six well-prodded daimyo petitioned: "Let the foolish argument be abandoned which has hitherto described the foreigners as dogs, goats and barbarians."

Other memorials followed, one reading:

> Since the Middle Ages our Emperor has lived behind a screen and has never trodden the earth. Nothing that went on outside his screen has penetrated his sacred ear; the Imperial Palace was secluded and outside the real world. Only a few court nobles were allowed to approach the throne, a practice most opposed to the principles of heaven. Although the first duty of man is to respect his superiors, if he reveres a superior too highly he neglects his duty, while a breach is created be-

tween the sovereign and his subjects, who are
unable to convey their wants to him. This vicious
practice has been common in all ages past. But
now let pompous etiquette be done away with,
and simplicity become our first object.

Representatives of foreign powers were soon told that
the Emperor had assumed control and that, in conformity
with Western diplomatic courtesy, he would be pleased to
grant them interviews. The unprecedented action created
a profound stir. Never before had a foreigner been allowed
to come into the presence of His Imperial Majesty!

But still there was bloodshed. The Dutch and French
ministers had completed official calls on the new Emperor
when ronin attacked the British minister as he journeyed to
the imperial palace. Manjiro's clansman, Goto Shojiro—an
expert swordsman accompanying the minister for protection—beheaded the assailant with one stroke. The Emperor
expressed profound regret and apologies for the attack, and
the interrupted call took place within a few days. With
little further delay the envoys succeeded in obtaining the
Emperor's signature to the treaties. Foreigners for the first
time realized that Japan had formerly been ruled by an
irreconcilable dualistic government.

The Emperor's Charter Oath, proclaimed in 1868, though
vague, was a tremendous first step toward constitutional
government. Perhaps most impressive to Manjiro—whose
good fortune it had been to be carried by the Pacific current
away from the shores of Japan during the enforcement of
the Exclusion Edict—was the fifth clause of this momentous
declaration: "Knowledge shall be sought throughout the
world, so that the welfare of the Empire may be promoted."
In its last years the Shogunate had sent a few select students
abroad for technical study and other eager youths had
gone secretly, but the Emperor now gave his approval. Japanese at last could openly travel and study abroad.

The new government was established at Yedo, the name of which was changed to Tokyo ("Eastern Capital"). Even the procession of the Emperor to his new seat of empire indicated change. Not long afterward Samuel C. Damon read in Honolulu a description of that significant event sent by an early teacher who had gone from the Islands to Japan:

It was regarded by the Japanese authorities as a remarkable concession to the common people, that, during the procession of the Mikado Emperor from the Southern capital to Yokohama, they were allowed to leave their houses as he passed by, also, in case of rain, to elevate their umbrellas. Hitherto when such journeys were made [referring to the Shogun] the doors of all the houses along the route were sealed up, and woe to the man who broke the seal, and went out while the sacred pageant was passing.

All Yokohama went to the place appointed to witness the spectacle. A multitude of natives lined the Tokaido. . . . Placards were put up in conspicuous places requesting the foreigners not to cheer when the Mikado passed. . . . We got a hint that his Majesty was approaching from the fact that the native officials came along and required of the Japanese, who lined the road, in places eight or ten deep, all to take down their hats and kneel down. . . . Soon the royal procession came in sight, headed by men on horseback, one after another, said to be Daimyos. Their saddles and bridles were richly ornamented. Their robes were very wide, and long and flowing, made of red and purple and yellow silk, with a profusion of rich ornaments. Those that followed on horseback, whether Daimyos or kuges, were all dressed in the same style, indicating that their rank was the same though their wealth was different. After the first two princes came companies of soldiers headed by

musicians playing ancient instruments. The tread
of all was completely noiseless.

About the center of the procession was the
closed chair of the Mikado richly ornamented and
surrounded by a large gold peacock [phoenix?];
but the curtains were drawn. It was borne very
slowly and solemnly by a number of uniformed
men wearing swords and at their sides walked
men of rank richly dressed. The high chair bore
the Mikado's crest and all eyes were strained to
pierce the curtains but to no avail. His Majesty
was as invisible as he would have been had we all,
after the maner of former days, been confined in
our houses, or he confined to his palace at Kyoto.
As he passed the Japanese were almost breathless
with awe and over all complete silence reigned.
All agreed it was a big step in advance of anything
yet witnessed in Japan.

Three months after the Emperor was established in the
new capital the various daimyo voluntarily gave up their
fiefs and were appointed governors, with greatly reduced
power and incomes; all their resources accrued to the
central government. By this act some 400,000 samurai now
became lordless. With an inherited disdain for money and
no business training, they found their small government
allotments wholly inadequate. Theirs was the greater sacrifice. Loyalty to a clan lord, basic in the samurai code of
honor, had now come to flower in national patriotism,
with the Emperor supreme.

Because the Bakufu had taken him from the Tosa
clan during the crisis occasioned by Perry's visit, Manjiro
also lost his position with the fall of the Shogunate. He
promptly returned to the service of the Tosa clan and represented it in Tokyo in consultations over policies of the new
government. He was also appointed a professor of second

rank in a school which in later amalgamation was to become the Imperial University (Kai-Sei Gakko).

Much as he enjoyed his new contacts, Manjiro soon resigned from his position. At forty-three years of age he felt his health required a rest from strenuous labor.

31

Return to Sconticut Neck

IN THE late summer of 1870 a government-sponsored delegation was organized to visit Europe. Its members were to observe the progress of the Franco-Prussian war and adapt the latest in military science to the needs of the rapidly expanding Japanese army.

Outstanding clan leaders had been chosen, and Manjiro was invited to accompany the group as official interpreter. He accepted, believing that a sea voyage would restore him to health. It was a stimulating company, including the man who was to become the illustrious Field Marshal Oyama, and Shinagawa Yajiro, afterward Minister of the Interior. Regrettably, Manjiro's fellow clansman, Itagaki Taisuke, was at the last moment detained in Tokyo. Three quarters of a century later Itagaki's likeness adorned the national currency in recognition of his illustrious career as a leader in the Restoration and his challenge when faced with assassination: "Though Itagaki may die, liberty will never be destroyed."

Just before sailing time the country learned that Napoleon III had surrendered, ending the war, but it was decided to proceed. The party left on September 24 by the American ship, *Great Republic,* and sailed directly to San Francisco. Manjiro was again impressed with the city's

216

growth. The delegation boarded trains for the trip across the continent. That had been made possible the year before when the Union Pacific—starting at the Missouri river at Omaha, Nebraska—met at Promontory, Utah, the Central Pacific—built from Sacramento, California—making a line 1,776 miles long. A stopover at Niagara Falls was a usual treat for sightseers. Amazing evidence of American progress was a newspaper called *The Transcontinental,* which was published daily on the train.

Most of the party looked forward to a five-day stay in New York as a great adventure, but to Manjiro the high point of the trip was a long-contemplated visit with Captain and Mrs. Whitfield in Fairhaven. He appeared unannounced at Sconticut Neck and was greeted with joyous exclamations of welcome. For the first time he met the stalwart young son and two lovely daughters, who plied him with questions and exclaimed over the gifts he had brought—fabulous silks, fans and lacquer ware which were astonishing evidence of Japan's leadership in many handcrafts.

Best of all to the visitor was the hour alone with the captain and his wife when they talked of times long past, days of joy and sorrow in the family circle. He was shown improvements within and without the home, none delighting him more than the pump over the kitchen sink which brought water from a well beneath the house. How vividly he remembered water-carrying days when, no matter how carefully balanced, the buckets would spill!

He observed less pleasant changes in the town itself. A hurricane the year before had destroyed well-remembered trees and the "Brick Church" had lost the spire that whalemen had long relied on as a beacon. Even the sturdy stone schoolhouse needed repair.

In Honolulu ten years before Manjiro had heard of the discovery of petroleum in Pennsylvania and with it gloomy forecasts of the future of the whale oil industry. Now, the captain told him, the industry, which had brought Fairhaven its prosperity for so long, was seriously crippled. The story of the Confederate raid on thirty-four whaling ships in the Arctic five years before was made real to him by the news that one of the ships captured and burned had been the *Favorite* of Fairhaven. The townspeople delighted to tell of Captain Young's defiance of the ruthless commander of the raiding *Shenandoah;* the fact that he had ended his cruise in irons did not detract from his heroism. Other ships whose names and rigs seemed familiar—the *Amazon,* the *Harvest* and *Rebecca Sims*—had been parts of the "Stone Fleet" which had been used in the ineffectual blockade of Charleston and Savannah harbors.

Sadly the veteran captain and his foster son wandered along the wharves, reconstructing their part in the robust past. Now the number of cruises decreased each year, and the old mill adjoining Fort Phoenix, once steadily in use for sharpening harpoons and blubber spades, often stood motionless. To a whaling community in which agriculture was only moderately profitable and manufacturing had not been introduced, the new situation brought consternation. Some prophesied that the oil wells would soon run dry, but to most people this seemed a false hope.

When they returned to Sconticut Neck, they found the house full of townsfolk, some of whom long before had objected to the attendance of the strange Japanese boy at their very exclusive churches. But attitudes had changed, and he was famous now. Eagerly they accepted the coins of his homeland as souvenirs. It was a happy time, to be remembered always. The only disappointment to the visitor was the absence of his old friend, Job Tripp. Later he discovered that he had passed Tripp at some distance and had failed to recognize him.

After Manjiro's departure Captain Whitfield wrote S. C. Damon in Honolulu:

> . . . John Mungero has made me a visit. He remembers you and all others that befriended him when he was poor. It is wonderful to see the workings of Providence, or of God, to bring about his ends . . . . Had he gone [home] at any other time he would have lost his life. He has retired from the Japanese navy and was living in the country, having ample means, when he was appointed with six others to visit the seat of war in Europe. He spells his name, as near as I can get it, Nokohama Mungero.

When the Japanese delegation reached London, Manjiro was too ill to proceed and it was agreed that he should return to Japan.

32

Wheels and More Wheels

WHEN Manjiro reached Yokohama early in 1871, he found a city he scarcely knew. Under the terms of the commercial treaty Kanagawa had been opened for foreign trade, but it had been surpassed in size and importance by Yokohama, now a great metropolis. The city sprawled over the swamps and contained numerous foreign houses on the "Bluff," numbered in the order in which they had been built without regard for future streets.

In the business section the usual crowds swarmed the thoroughfares, itinerant merchants with their wares slung over shoulder poles; ox carts lumbered by and there were great numbers of a recently introduced vehicle to which the name *jinrikisha* had been given. These two-wheeled, usually single-seated conveyances—which some jestingly called "pull-man cars"—were drawn by brawny, barelegged men who resembled the cross-country runners of old but who had made some concessions in the matter of clothing. The constant cries of these men brought a strident note to the monotonous undertone of the streets. Western vehicles had also invaded the country. Wheels and more wheels! They were everywhere!

Hidden away in tiny shops in the native quarter were beautiful silks, lacquer ware, bronzes and carvings. Foreign merchants brazenly displayed stoves, cutlery, clocks, buttons, matches, perfumed soap, bowler hats, fancy waistcoats, condensed milk, bottled beer and pictures of George Washington, Napoleon and Bismarck. There were many photograph galleries, where strange men posed with once-demure girls who had been sold to brothels by destitute parents. Mingling with the natives were French soldiers in blue and Britishers in red coats. Nowhere in his travels had Manjiro seen such a heterogeneous scene.

Long experience with the subservient Dutch had ill prepared the Japanese for business dealings with traders who claimed the rights of equals. Traditionally they hated foreigners, and to be forced into association with them on the level of traders was to many a degrading experience. Swaggering foreigners, on the other hand, completely discounted Japanese spirit and rules of conduct, classifying all nationals as either vacillating or stupid. These men were often adventurers without honor in their own countries. To cheat and browbeat seemed part of their natures. In self-defense the Japanese placed every possible obstacle in the way of smooth operation of the treaties and often resorted to the old trick of causing loss of face by forcing the foreigners to deal with underlings instead of those in authority. Ill will as well as a new civilization was building.

The rice economy of twenty years before was a thing of the past. New coins from seemingly every country in the world circulated; in some notorious transactions it was said they were weighed pound for pound to the disadvantage of the Japanese.

Equally sinister was international speculation in Japanese gold. Deserting legitimate trade, officers on foreign ships bought quantities of the precious metal and shipped it to China with a hundred percent profit. A struggling government unused to high finance seemed unable to find a solution to the problem of dwindling national resources.

Two years before, the lord of the Tosa clan had presented Manjiro with a charming villa in Tokyo, which now became a welcome retreat. Manjiro had remarried, and his new wife's care and nursing soon brought relief from the leg ulcers which had plagued him during his trip; the joy of being with his children once more—there were four now—completed the cure. On his estate of six acres was a pond which drew wild ducks, and Toichiro was permitted to shoot them when accompanied by his father. Manjiro could now thoroughly enjoy his long-interrupted family life. New friends came to him, too, for instruction in English or to hear him tell of his experiences in whaling. These were old stories by now, but they always fascinated new groups.

Despite all difficulties, the country was making rapid progress. Some mourned for the old, time-honored values which seemed things of the past. The industrial revolution had not only changed the thoughts and tempo of the nation but was sweeping away the integrity of craftsmanship. Many a master in the creative arts, knowing that consecration and painstaking work could not be demanded merely by money, was confronted with the nightmare of hurry. Higher prices, cheaper goods, a lowering of standards—these left life meaningless for many.

Too, the rigid class system of the past was falling apart. Before they were aware of it lordly samurai owed money to lowly merchants. Normally preferring near starvation to association with those considered beneath them, hard-pressed men now frequently defiled the family name by marrying their daughters to those who held the moneybags.

These were not Manjiro's own problems but they touched him because they brought to light the deep distress of the country. He took time to counsel his friends on the role of the individual in the mass upheaval.

He was better trained in handiwork and expediency than most of the samurai who were suddenly thrown on their own resources, but he was physically unable to enter the whirl of competitive business or to return to the rigorous work of whaling. He was wistfully aware that the government was importing foreign experts in great numbers. These specialists were called *yatoi,* meaning "hired helpers," and some made contributions of lasting value to Japan. They were usually chosen for the special abilities of the countries they represented—education and postal specialists from the United States; medical men from Germany; military experts from France; engineering, railway and telegraph consultants from England. From the semiobscurity of his home Manjiro followed the building of railroads, lighthouses, sanitary systems—watched Japan change her face.

The government, however, stubbornly resisted the reform relating to religious freedom. A government mission headed by the high-ranking patriot, Iwakura Tomomi, toured many countries with the hope of revising the unequal treaties. Proud Japan could no longer accept the fact that all foreigners in their land were under the jurisdiction of their own consular courts, which placed Japan in an inferior position in the eyes of the world. The mission was welcomed most cordially in Washington and other capitals of the world but was told bluntly that for the present there could be no change in the situation.

An incident brought to public attention by an American missionary from Hawaii finally made it clear that religious persecution was blocking Japan's demands. The Reverend Orramel H. Gulick, the first missionary under the American Board in Japan, had employed as his teacher of the Japanese language a certain Ichikawa Einosuke. When the authorities heard that together they were translating parts of the New Testament into Japanese, they arrested Ichikawa in the dead of night and thrust him into prison. His wife was imprisoned also because she had "shared his sin." The missionary called on the Japanese authorities to plead the

man's innocence, and learned that if Ichikawa had accepted
Christian baptism he could not escape the death penalty.
The American minister in Tokyo warned that this ill treatment of Christians would affect the friendly relations of the
United States and Japan, and this was confirmed wherever
the Iwakura Mission traveled. The story of Ichikawa's mis-
treatment was known in official circles everywhere, and all
Christian countries concurred in the opinion that Japan
must mend her ways before desired changes in the treaties
could be granted. Soon after the return of the Iwakura
Mission in 1873, the ban on Christianity was removed and
the old edict boards came down.

Another disability struck Manjiro without warning. It
was a paralytic stroke which left his speech thick and one
side of his body useless. But with remarkable vitality he
soon began to recover. For complete quiet he was moved to
Kamakura where his son Toichiro had built a home. Toichiro was a medical student under German professors, and
with his devoted care the father continued to improve.

After several months he was able to visit his mother.
Two years later he made another trip to Nakanohama, this
time taking Toichiro. It was the first time the young man
had seen his grandmother. He arrived at her home wan from
seasickness, a malady which Manjiro had never experienced
and with which he found it difficult to sympathize. Toichiro
visited the near-by Buddhist temple to see the stone which
had been placed as a memorial to his father when he failed
to return from that long-ago fishing expedition.

To Manjiro the whole atmosphere of the village had
changed. The commercial value of the exceptionally beautiful coral discovered in surrounding waters had brought
prosperity to the province, along with its already famous,
fine handmade paper. Manjiro tried angling in the familiar
waters and exultantly caught two large perch.

At Kochi, the capital, Toichiro was surprised to see men with their hair dressed in the old topknot style and with swords at their sides. The practice of carrying swords had fallen into disuse with the demotion of the samurai, and the following year it was to be officially abolished. This isolated province displayed unlooked-for rebellion against the arbitrary ways of the Meiji government. Toichiro also noticed that the old clan currency was in use.

The parting with his mother was most affecting to Manjiro since she had a premonition that she would never see him or her grandson again. Four years later she died during a cholera epidemic.

Two Visitors and a Kabuki Play

ISABELLA BIRD toured Japan in 1878 preparatory to writing her well-known book, *Unbeaten Tracks in Japan*. Samuel C. Damon, who had met Miss Bird while she was in Honolulu at work on her *Six Months in the Sandwich Islands*, wrote her concerning Manjiro and asked her to look him up if possible. She replied to his request for information on November 16, 1879, from her home in Edinburgh:

> . . . Now I must tell you about your last letter. Strange to say I received The Friend with an account of the Ainos in Yezo the day before I left for a three weeks tour among the Ainos, and consequently it interested me greatly, as did those truly pathetic aborigines. I had previously become very well acquainted with Mr. and Mrs. Murray, and on returning to Tokyo lost no time in speaking to them about Mangero and Mr. Murray took a great deal of time to find him out, and having done so, invited him to meet me at lunch. Mangero is quite an old-looking and sad-looking man. His party is out of power and himself out of employment, and he lives on a plot of land some distance from Tokyo. He brightened very much

226

when he heard of you, and especially when I gave him your photo and message. I urged him to write to you, but he has nearly forgotten English. Your thought of him seemed to be quite a gleam of brightness in his depressed condition, and I am glad you gave me the message to find him.

Manjiro's seeming depression was largely due to ill health and the fact that he was no longer able to share in the development of his country. Actually he enjoyed great freedom, living at times with his son in Kamakura, again in Tokyo, and occasionally at Atami Hot Springs, where he found the baths helpful.

His son tells of his good works: his kindness to the ill and poor— "Whenever a beggar came to the gate he was given a bowl of rice"—his encouragement to a struggling young artist who had studied oil painting at Nagasaki and was meeting with little appreciation since the new medium was not understood; his gallant spirit in always taking the weaker side; his abhorrence of false display and ceremony; his adherence to the truth; his frugality; his quiet courage. Those who observed Manjiro's way of life often said he had "the universal heart."

In 1881, when Manjiro's exploits in the Western world were only a memory, King Kalakaua of Hawaii visited Tokyo on the first lap of a world tour. A reciprocity treaty between the United States and Hawaii had greatly stimulated the production of sugar, and the Islands discovered an acute need for plantation laborers. Japan was a logical source of supply.

The authorities knew that the removal of the extraterritoriality clause in the 1871 treaty between Hawaii and Japan would greatly please Japan, and very soon the proposed revision was agreed on as evidence of good will. The

King instructed the Commissioner of Immigration, who had accompanied him on the tour, to confer further in the matter.

Aided and abetted by Walter Murray Gibson, a foreign adventurer in his court, the King had a grandiose plan to bring Hawaii and Japan into a federation which would make him one of a group of Asiatic Princes and greatly extend both his influence and population. Kalakaua made his proposal at a secret meeting with the Meiji Emperor and further embroidered the idea with the proposal of a marriage between his young niece and a fifteen-year-old hereditary prince then attending a naval training school in Tokyo.

But the Japanese government realized that the King did not speak for the American element in the Islands. The government knew too that the United States was the most likely of world powers to befriend Japan in the hoped-for general treaty revision. Politely the official representatives rejected both the federation and matrimonial alliance.

But after considerable diplomatic dispute emigratory laws were established. Once the bars were down, people remembered Manjiro's description of Hawaii's agricultural opportunities: "The climate is so favorable that crops come up all the year around," and other later favorable reports. Emigration from Japan was soon in full tide.

Samuel C. Damon had long wished to visit Japan. The opportunity came after he had officiated at the marriage of his son Frank to the daughter of an American missionary in China. Accompanying him was his wife, also seeing the Orient for the first time. The venerable editor was almost ready to retire; in his "valedictory," he recalled that his active service during the better part of a half century covered the full reigns of three Hawaiian kings, and parts of two others. In 1842 when he arrived at the port of Honolulu as seamen's chaplain, California had been under Mexican rule, and the town of San Francisco "was wont to derive her news of the outside world via Honolulu. There was not an English newspaper printed on the western coast of North or South America from Cape Horn to Bering Strait, or in any part of Polynesia." Many of the children of California pioneers had been sent to Honolulu to school, and the same slow sailing ships had carried family laundry back and forth.

So valuable had *The Friend* become that the British Museum had requested a complete file, as had George Bancroft to document parts of his *History of the United States*. The full reports of the whaling fleet and early accounts of the discovery of gold in California and Australia were particularly sought. "It affords satisfaction that this little sheet has cheered the cabins and forecastles of vessels as they have cruised the Pacific waters and Arctic seas" was the editor's concluding comment.

His report on Manjiro ended the saga of the shipwrecked Japanese which he had begun over three decades before in the same newspaper:

> ... We are happy to state that our desire to locate Manjiro was fully gratified and we found our friend the father of a most promising family numbering four sons and one daughter. He presented us with photographs of his wife and interesting family. His oldest son is now a physician of much promise, and engaged in one of the government hospitals of southeastern Japan. Another son is an educated architect. He came with his sons from Tokio to Yokohama, to bid us farewell. Long shall we cherish the memory of our visit to Japan, but among the most pleasing incidents of that visit were the repeated interviews with Nakahama Manjiro, the wrecked sailor-boy, the successful adventurer in returning to his native land and the translator of Bowditch's Navigator. He informed us that he has in his possession a single

copy of this translation, and we have a copy presented by him in 1860.* No other copies are
known to be in existence, all having been destroyed in the conflagration in Tokio, when some
government buildings were burned with the archives of Japan.

He is about sixty years of age, but not possessed
of a large amount of this world's goods, being dependent upon his sons for support. We most sincerely wish the Japanese government might honor
itself by honoring its old and faithful servant with
a liberal pension. Long may he live and prosper.

The Japanese theater remained aloof from revolutionary change until the year 1888. The classical *No* drama, for
centuries the stately entertainment of the court and nobility, had lost none of its religious and aesthetic appeal.
But a new departure in the *Kabuki-za* (Theater) forced
it finally from traditional dancing and posturing, with
orchestral recitative, to realistic speech and action. Many
thought the new form coarse and even lewd.

When the *Shintomi-za* in Tokyo announced by means of
huge posters the showing of a new drama titled *Tosa Han-
shi Hatsunibune,* by the playwright Takeshiba Kisui, there
was consternation in the Nakahama household. *Tosa Han-
shi* referred to the traditional first shipload of Tosa paper, a
dramatic event of each New Year; it pointed indirectly to
the well-known Tosa man who had first brought them word
of life in the United States, Manjiro without doubt. Sadanji,
an actor of a famous hereditary line, depicted him as a man
of many facets, most disturbingly as a frequenter of the
gay quarters at Uraga known as Kameya and an associate
of courtesans.

---

* Manjiro's two-volume work so prized by the veteran editor was
lost after his death, which occurred the year after his retirement.

Toichiro was in Germany completing a postgraduate course in medicine, and his half-brother Keizaburo—destined to become paymaster of the Japanese cruiser *Kasagi*, built at Philadelphia—had been charged with the care of his father. He grew more and more indignant as he heard the story of the drama.

Manjiro himself was complacent. He had experienced too many disturbing realities to concern himself with anything that was pure fiction. Besides, had he not completed the coveted cycle of lunar years and entered upon a changed phase of existence? He was sixty-one and he could accept this as part of the new order.

The play was melodramatic, opening in the Seiryuji temple as Manjiro's mother and sister offered prayers on the thirteenth anniversary of his death. Close to the latter-day technique of Hollywood, it progressed from reverential Buddhistic worship to scenes of the underworld and, finally, to a wrestling match in which a Japanese won from an American Negro. The curtain went down during the tumultuous acclaim of the champion.

The fisherman's son who had attained fame was a perfect character for such a play, and the popularity of Sadanji gave it immediate success. Manjiro decided to see it. Previously a samurai had not been allowed to enter a *kabuki* theater, but many now went without question. Besides, Manjiro's independent spirit brooked no interference. Accompanied by a young retainer,* who guided his faltering steps whenever he ventured from home, he made his way to the crowded theater. Almost immediately he was recognized and given a seat of honor in the center of the audience. Between scenes the actors filed down the raised walk leading from the stage to pay their respects to the surviving hero.

---

* Now Mrs. Kuni Kaneko of Tokyo, who tells the story.

The engagement had long been completed when Toi-chiro, then a graduate doctor, returned from abroad. To satisfy his curiosity, he read the play and decided that his father had been right in not resenting it.

The play, now hidden away in the archives of the drama department of Waseda University, while extravagant, contains a germ of truth. It perhaps answers better than anything else the twentieth-century question: *Why was Manjiro not assassinated by a fanatical patriot of his time?* In the third act his wife—by inference a beautiful courtesan—overhears a group of lordless samurai discussing the deplorable condition of the country. They charge Manjiro, the returned traveler, with responsibility, and blame Commissioner Hayashi for formulating treaties with the foreigners. They decide finally to kill them both.

But Manjiro's wife tells him of the plan, and he sends her to warn Hayashi. He assumes personal responsibility for teaching his countrymen how to know and appreciate America, even at the risk of his life.

In a later scene he boldly appears before his accusers and exclaims, "If you have good reason to kill me, I am willing to die!" In answer to the accusation that his duplicity had brought the Americans to Uraga, he declares boldly that he had never heard of Perry until his ships arrived in Japan. He also explains Western conditions as he has personally seen them and justifies Hayashi's part in the formulation of the treaties, explaining that only by such statesmanship was the country to be saved from foreign attack. He further emphasizes the need for strengthening Japan's army and navy and urges concerted effort to bring the country under a just, single rule. The lordless samurai are now convinced that Manjiro has fulfilled his *giri* (or sacred obligation), that his arguments are sound and that his advice should be followed. He gives them money with which to go home, and they disperse quietly.

Was it not his fearlessness, the timeliness of his advice and the reasonableness of his approach that saved Manjiro from his enemies?

Just as these good qualities stood between him and the violence of those who hated what he had brought to pass, so his modesty and unostentatious manner kept much of his contribution from being widely known and quickly appreciated. Manjiro's death on November 12, 1898, was not an occasion for national mourning. Only time, recognizing his gifts to Japan, pays its tribute.

Epilogue

Now an octogenarian, Mrs. Kuni Kaneko of Tokyo, Manjiro's faithful domestic from the time she was fifteen until his death, still remembers his delight in playing *Tokaido Sugoroku* with his grandchildren in the long winter evenings. The game promoted skill in dice throwing and helped keep alive the old place names. On a large card placed on the floor in the center of the group were pictures of the fifty-three post stations between Tokyo and Kyoto. A few coins or a pile of cakes marked the last station, which was the old capital. Each throw of dice advanced the players toward the goal, excitement increasing with each lap of the imaginary journey.

Manjiro's memories were keen, and often he enlivened the hour before bedtime with stories of the colorful folk life he had witnessed when, as a fearful youth, he had traveled these difficult miles on his way to Yedo at the call of the Bakufu—deep chasms which had to be crossed in bamboo baskets swung on fiber cables and other hazards of the journey.

When the laughter had died and each child had made his respectful bow to the venerable *Ojii San,* Manjiro would often doze, a smile lighting up his wrinkled face. There the picture fades . . .

Memories! How they crowd upon the old, and what a panorama they presented to the mind of this man who had gone so far from his native tides! The rescue from impending death on a barren rock in the sea; the friendly aloha of a towering Hawaiian chief; school days in New

England; carefree months when taut sails carried him to strange places and stranger peoples; the quest for gold; reunion with his mother; summons by the Bakufu; the disappointment of not being present when the great commodore negotiated with the officials; the unswerving friendship of two fine Americans. These were deeply etched on his mind.

Japan's swift political and industrial progress—astonishing in the eyes of the world—had been too rapid for complete understanding, and the removal of the ban against foreign travel had released minds long undernourished. The impetus of these forces was making Japan into the first country in Asia to have a literate population.

The elevation of a million outcasts to Japanese citizenship was as revolutionary as the freeing of slaves in America. Only eleven short years lay between official permission for commoners to take surnames and the imperial decree promising the convention of a national assembly; only eight more before the promulgation of the first constitution. The first parliament of Japan had been opened in 1889 by the Emperor in person, and the year following his famous Rescript on Education was issued.

Manjiro had personally known most of the men who struggled and sacrificed for these developments, and he followed their careers with pride. But deeper than admiration was his affectionate regard for Goto Shojiro, who was to be remembered always as his first pupil, and Kawada Shoryu, the artist who had recorded his travels in strange lands and copied his world map at the order of their clan lord. Goto was one of a group of samurai, including Itagaki Taisuku, who addressed a memorial to the Meiji government demanding the early establishment of a representative assembly. And Kawada was said to have inspired his clansman, Sakamoto Ryuma, with the idea of a Diet system. Sakamoto had also worked toward the overthrow of the

Shogunate; after the Restoration he had taken an important post in the new government, only to be assassinated at last for his liberal views. With him worked Katsu Awa, who was successful in arranging the surrender of Yedo Castle to the imperial forces. Katsu had become the first Minister of the Navy. As the organizer of a great shipping company, first known as the Mitsu Bishi, Iwasaki Yataro was already a figure of international importance.

Through the combined efforts of such men Japan had become a progressive nation founded on the principles of democracy. Through many of them the ancient oracle had been fulfilled: *From the land of Tosa freedom shall flow!*

That it was Manjiro, the Tosa fisherman, who had blazed the trail it remained for another century to discover.

Appendixes and Index

Appendixes

I. DISCOVERY OF THE ORIGINAL MANUSCRIPTS OF MANJIRO'S STORY

(Written for the *Morning Mercury* of Fairhaven, Massachusetts, July 4, 1918, by Stewart Culin, Curator, Brooklyn Museum)

On my last visit to Japan in 1912, an expedition which I made in behalf of the Brooklyn Museum, I purchased, while buying Japanese books for my library, an illustrated manuscript report made by Nakahama Manjiro, describing his rescue by Captain Whitfield and his life subsequently in America. I found the work at an exhibition and sale of the second-hand booksellers of Tokyo at the house of the Tokyo Fine Arts Society near the *Ryogokubashi*. Many thousand volumes were spread out on the mats of the enormous exhibition room, each dealer's stock being arranged by itself on the floor. Sitting down among the piles my hand fell upon four bound volumes illustrated with pictures [some of which were] in water color referring to New England. I bought them without further examination and called on my artist friend, Kataoka Senjiro, known in America under his artist name of Yeto as the illustrator of some of Hearn's stories, and had Mr. Kataoka translate the manuscript. It proved to be a first-hand copy, written at Manjiro's dictation by an artist in the employ of the Lord of Tosa and made, no doubt, by the order of that personage. It contained a detailed account of the rescue of Manjiro and his companions by Captain Whitfield. This was followed by the story of Manjiro's voyage home to Fairhaven with Captain Whitfield, his life there, his trips on whaling voyages, his journey to California, where he dug gold and obtained money to go home, and his return at last to Japan by the way of the Sandwich Islands. The story of his residence in Fairhaven was told in great detail and with an intimate and affectionate mention of those who befriended him, and was illustrated with signed pictures [some of which were] drawn by Manjiro showing all of the common objects, strange to him, that he saw for the first time. He told in minute detail, with maps, all about his whaling voyage, with pictures of the ship and the things connected with it down to the portrait of his [the captain's] wife, which the captain kept in his cabin. There is a sketch of Fairhaven, represented as a very dreamlike Chinese villa, and of the city of Boston, the latter a charming work of art in which fact is well mixed with fancy. His shipwrecked companions were not neglected and he records many details about their life in Hawaii while he was in New England being educated and planning for their return home. This return which he arranged and paid for is set down with great modesty, as is also the story of his experiences in Japan down to the time of the report. There is a whimsical title page written in English by Manjiro reading, "The Story of Four Japanese."

It happened that during my visit an exhibition of relics of Manjiro was given by Professor Shiga, the eminent Japanese geographer, at the Imperial Hotel in Tokyo. This led to my acquaintance with this charming man. Up to that time I assumed that the report I purchased in Tokyo was one of many, as it was customary to reproduce such books, but Professor Shiga declared it new to him. Subsequent search in Japanese libraries failed to reveal any reference to it or to any other copy. Its possession led to my meeting Dr. Nakahama, Manjiro's son, who called upon me and examined the manuscript. "My beloved father's hand!" he exclaimed. "Surely this is the work of God." The report was unknown to him, and I lent it to him to copy the parts that were unfamiliar, while he in turn wrote for me an account of his father's career in Japan to embody in the publication I contemplated. Professor Shiga also gave me copies of the data he had collected. I myself set to work to collect everything I could find relative to Manjiro, the story of his adventures in America having excited great interest at home [Japan] and led to the publication of little books which purported to be authentic. The interest and value of the narrative became more and more apparent and I again visited Japan, stopping in Hawaii in search of material, and then continuing my efforts there and here until some of the obscure points in the original text were cleared up. Proper names, in many cases, were difficult to identify, and some of the names of Hawaiians remain unsolved. In the course of my search I found other stories of Japanese shipwrecked in America, all of which I have followed in the way here related. All of them are interesting, but none have the simplicity—the fine quality of Manjiro Nakahama's story. It is a record of which both Japan and America may be proud. Fidelity, courage and loyalty have fewer brighter examples and have seldom received a more just reward.

II. MEMORIAL SWORD PRESENTED
TO FAIRHAVEN

The town of Fairhaven, Massachusetts, was gay with bunting and festive throngs on July 4, 1918. The occasion was the formal presentation of an ancient samurai sword to the town by Dr. Toichiro Nakahama of Tokyo in grateful memory of the rescue of his father, Nakahama Manjiro, and his education before the establishment of public schools in America.

*Following are the personal memories of Mrs.
Charles S. Hamlin, whose late husband as governor of the Federal Reserve Board, helped to ar-
range the event.*

Viscount Ishii headed the Japanese commission that
came to Washington in 1917 after we had entered World
War I. My husband told him the story of Manjiro and his
life with the Whitfields and the Viscount stated that he
would take up the matter of a suitable celebration with his
government even though it was war time.

The following winter he returned to Washington as
Ambassador, and on the day of his arrival he telephoned
and invited us both to come to the Embassy that same afternoon as he had something to show us. The Embassy at that
time was a large, gloomy old house on McPherson Square,
but that afternoon it looked cheerful with flowers and
Madam Ishii to welcome us. She gave us Japanese tea, beautifully served. The Ambassador then showed us the present
he had brought with him from the son of Manjiro for the
town of Fairhaven. It was a beautifully wrought Samurai
sword. I think my husband was as surprised as I was at the
selection. I ventured on the question, "Why a sword?" The
Ambassador explained that from the Japanese point of
view it stood for the highest honor and chivalry.

From that time on plans for the celebration developed.
Mayor Ashley of New Bedford came down to talk it over
with the Ambassador. He also represented the Selectmen
and a special committee of Fairhaven. All were acting
together to make a successful celebration.

President Wilson had felt that this celebration was of
such importance in the happy relations of the two countries
that he had excused the Ambassador from the usual meeting
of diplomats at Mount Vernon on July 4th.

The Ambassador and Madam Ishii were to be our houseguests at Mattapoisett, our summer home near Fairhaven. With them came the military attaché, Colonel Tanakawa, a distinguished man with many medals. He was a victim the following October of the deadly "flu" which swept the country. The State Department sent a Secret Service man, Mr. Candee.

Arriving with the guests was a large glass case for the sword. When it was unpacked the acute eye of the Ambassador discovered a small crack in one corner. It was really too small to be noticed and it was suggested that it could be repaired after the celebration. But this was vetoed at once; it must not be presented unless it was in perfect order.

In order to enliven the waiting time after breakfast the next morning my husband explained that we were living on a small farm and that it was a Yankee custom for everyone to help bring in the hay. So we all went out into the hot sun. Rakes were provided, and all, including the Ambassador in his top hat and frock coat, worked energetically. Someone spoke of our litter of pigs three days old and the Ambassador enjoyed the sport of giving them a cooling bath with a hose.

When Madam Ishii joined us at lunch she wore a lovely gray costume fit for Newport. She said she had brought a Japanese costume, and this seemed a good chance to say how much I admired the beautiful native dress, and how much I would be pleased if she would wear it at the afternoon reception we had planned. The Ambassador remarked, "That is different," in a grave voice so we did not know until she came down stairs about four o'clock whether she would wear it or not. But they had decided in favor of it and it was a lovely costume of soft greenish gray. She was greatly worried because she did not have the correct sandals or slippers, but she looked right to us and made a charming picture.

The State Department had sent us two large Japanese flags. One of them hung with the Stars and Stripes from our flag pole and the other was raised over the Town Hall. Twice during the reception Mr. Candee asked in an undertone if I knew an approaching man. One was good old Ezra Bridgham who habitually talked to himself. He was excited that day and talked very loud. He kept repeating, "A real Ambassyder—think of shaking hands." As he stood opposite he reached out his hand and swung the Ambassador's arm back and forth, saying, "Say, you look like anyone else. I belong to the Moose Order, Sir. Now I can tell them that I shook hands with a real Ambassyder."

The other man was a character from East Mattapoisett known as Bub Roger Dexter. He carried a large brown paper bundle—probably his supper—and to the Secret Service representative looked suspicious. He was very polite, shook hands gravely and passed along without incident.

Fully three hundred people turned out that lovely afternoon. The Delanos were at the Homestead at that time and many Washington friends from Nonquitt motored over.

It seemed that everyone in town was out waving as we sped in motors to the celebration the next morning. It was another perfect day and the Fairhaven bridge was a sight to see. Japanese and American flags waved from every lamp post. At street corners school children waved and shouted "Banzai! Banzai!" The Mayor presided over the exercises at the High School and Acting-Governor Calvin Coolidge gave the address of welcome. The Ambassador's speech was very fine. Mrs. Ishii was also called upon to speak, but she smiled and bowed instead.

At the Old Whaling Museum we were welcomed at the large door on Johnny Cake Hill. In the new wing the half-sized model of the whaleship *Lagoda* lay in all her beauty.

Before lunch at Tabitha Inn Ambassador Ishii reverently

placed a large wreath of roses on Captain Whitfield's grave. We visited the house where Nakahama first stayed with the Whitfields, then went to see an old lady whose mother had been in the house when he first arrived. Visits to the Millicent Library and the Town Hall followed. At the first the Samurai sword was to be permanently kept, and at the latter a painting of the *John Howland,* the ship Captain Whitfield commanded at the time of Nakahama's rescue, was on display.

The sword was formally accepted at the Fairhaven High School. By happy good fortune Mr. Whitfield, the grandson of Captain Whitfield, was one of the Selectmen and he held his boy of five years in his arms during the presentation. It was an unusual scene.

Viscount Ishii was Japanese Ambassador to France and also represented Japan at the League of Nations in Geneva. It was there that we saw him and his wife again in the fall of 1925. In later years he came alone to Washington and had luncheon with President Roosevelt at the White House. They talked about the Fairhaven celebration and later the President wrote a personal letter to Dr. Nakahama in Tokyo in which he recalled his Fairhaven memories.

III. TEXT OF A LETTER WRITTEN AT THE RYUKYU ISLANDS BY CAPTAIN GEORGE E. WELCH, COMMANDING THE AMERICAN BARK *MERLIN*

(Published in *The Friend,* Honolulu, S. I., February 1851)

To the Regent and Other High and Illustrious Mandarins of the Loo Choo:

In regard to the edict by which I am ordered by you to take the fire-ship under my command and sail away from the shores of Loo Choo, I beg leave to state, that I came to your Island because on the 27th of the present moon (December, 1850) I fell in with a strong and mighty typhoon, which disabled my ship and caused it to leak so badly as to come near sinking in the depth of the Japan Sea. I passed many Islands because the inhabitants of them were not known by Christians, but as your Island had been famed far and wide for the wisdom and kindness of its people, I sought the shelter of its shores, with confidence that I would be allowed to repair my damages unmolested. I did not leave my anchorage in accordance with your edict because I considered it mere form and believed that you had too much good will and generosity to carry out its requirements, and even if you had chosen to do so I had on board my ship fire guns both big and small and many sailors with hearts and hands to use them, in order to repel aggression. Since your quiet and tacit consent to my remaining to complete my repairs I feel obliged to return my sincere thanks for your extreme kindness and consideration to myself and those under my command.

The presents you have sent me are very acceptable, and I trust that those I send in return, may be equally so to yourselves. I wish you to understand, however, that I shall not accept any more unless you consent to receive pay for them, because you might on my leaving, stigmatize us as coming from a nation of beggars. Neither the American or English, as nations, are considered beggars; on the contrary their mighty power is felt all over the world, and when you taunt the Christian missionary by telling him that they are beggars, you do rank injustice to friendly nations, and also to your own character for shrewdness and foresight. After taking my dimensions the other day some of you were pleased to flatter me by saying that I must be in battle a mighty warrior; in my country are many warriors, with a fame and glory so high that mine could not be seen in the glare of the noonday sun. How terrible then would be the vengeance that aggression would bring down on the heads of those who offend such rulers. Some of you have said that any favor I may ask, in your power to grant, shall be conceded to me. I have only to remark (hoping that I may receive attention) that the English government has placed on your Island a Christian missionary. He complains that you misuse him, bamboo him in the street, and starve him, his wife and little ones. He is a learned and wise man, and also a medical chief, understands and teaches almost all the languages of the earth, and administers to the diseases of both body and mind, and although as a Christian missionary, he is not allowed to fight like a Tartar, still his words are always heavy, and will go farther and weigh more, in some cases, even than the warrior with his ship and fire guns. Any injury or insult you may do him will surely be repaid ten fold. Even now English fire ships, with their big guns, are prowling about your coast—the smallest of which, in one hour could destroy your populous city and make the beautiful burial place of your fathers a disgusting and sightless wilderness. If, as you seem to think, his doctrines are wrong and absurd, surely the superior wisdom the Japanese lay claim to, will prevent their having an undue influence. If right, as I trust you will soon find them, you will have a great cause to regret having injured one who has been working long and faithfully for your good. I have offered to take him from your Island, but he declines. He would sooner die than leave his post without orders, surely the courage of such a man should command respect and reverence, instead of wrong and injury. He also complains that the food which you furnish him with makes him sick, and that you allow snakes to hiss and quarter in the sleeping places of his children, and in endeavoring to destroy them you deter him from so doing. If you continue to treat him in this manner I shall consider it my duty to report it to his government, and they will not fail to find a reason for the different manner in which you treat those who come in fire ships, and him who extends a peace offering. I shall not fail to report to my government the kind and generous treatment I have received at your hands. I beg leave to repeat to your Excellencies my thanks for your kindness, and wishing you numberless moons of happiness and prosperity, I subscribe myself,

Your ob't servant

GEORGE E. WELCH
Master Bark Merlin

IV. INFORMATION GIVEN AT
NAGASAKI TRIALS

For greater comprehensiveness the testimony is here grouped according to geographical location.

Sandwich Islands:

The islands have a uniform climate throughout the year. It is warm but not unbearable. The natives wear summer clothing at all times. We never experienced earthquakes or thunder.

The port opens to the south.

A revenue of 120,000 gold represents the tax collected from ships of every country.

A king governs these islands. When he dies he is put in a coffin narrow at the bottom, and a ceremony is made for the dead. The coffin is stored in a fire-proof place like a go-down. Common people are buried in the ground.

The houses are thatched with grass. Americans developed this country and they are now teaching the people to cover their houses with plank.

The hut at the fort in which we lived belonged to a minor official. The uprights were of wood called hau, resembling paulownia. On the floor was a matlike covering made of woven grass resembling miscanthus growing on the river banks. There are many trees such as the hau and the bead tree. There are no trees well known in Japan such as the pine, Chinese black pine, oak, plum and cherry trees.

Meals were served three times a day by official order and consisted of something like a dumpling made from taro and sweet potato, steamed and mashed. We also had chicken, pork, and fish parched with salt.

Unseasoned wood was used in building fires for cooking. Ladles were made of coconut.

There were many birds quite unknown in Japan. Soya beans and Indian beans were not grown, but flat beans looking like kidney beans were planted.

Sugar canes were grown extensively. The stem of this plant reaches a height of six or seven feet. After being harvested sugar canes were sent to other islands where Chinese workers processed the sugar. Sugar, dry and of good quality, brown and white, in color, was sent to other countries.

Cotton is also grown. Leaves and flowers are similar to Japanese cotton. The fibers are soft and white but they are not woven into cloth, but are used for stuffing bedding.

Every month throughout the year there are four holidays. There are two temple-like churches. One of them has a hanging bell. The floor is paved with stone and has many benches. The bell is to call the people at 10 A.M. on each holiday. When men and women, old and young, gather there is a person who appears to be the master. He wears woolen clothes with narrow sleeves, and teaches the people to be diligent in their occupation and to observe the moral code. Though we attended the meetings we could not understand what was preached.

On Oahu the females are very much like Japanese women. They wore tortoise shell pins in their hair and also flowers picked from the roadside. Women looking like prostitutes adorned their hair with many ornaments and wore fine clothes. There was a gay quarter.

When the American residents sleep they go into a place like a cupboard. They dislike to have people see them while sleeping.

The United States:

The country is opening up gradually and learning is constantly becoming greater. America is working to develop its own country and has no time to attack other countries.

The character of the people is very generous and honest and they do little wrong. Cases of murder and robbery are scarce.

Punishment is very just, but when a murderer is caught he pays with his life. If there is any doubt about his crime a public vote is taken.

There is only one era since the country started. The year is divided into twelve months. Four months have thirty days, seven have thirty-one and one month has twenty-eight days. Every fourth year there is one month which consists of twenty-nine days. There is no such thing as tiger year, rat year, dragon, wild boar, etc. There are twenty-four hours in a day. Owing to differences in the calendars, October in Japan would be November over there. Americans do not calculate their ages like the Japanese and a baby born in November of any year is reckoned one year old at the end of twelve months, instead of two years old after January first of the next year.

The principle of counting is much the same but their *abacus* is different. It is a piece of thick purple stone a foot square with a wooden frame. They count by inscribing numerals with what looks like a nail. When it is wiped with the fingers, numerals all disappear.

In the United States they call a temple a church. The priest dresses like a common man. He has a wife and children and they all eat meat. Churches are large and often have a clock on the tower. There are no Buddhist images. Many people gather with their books and the priest stands on a high platform and tells the people to open their books at certain pages. The priest reads from these pages and then explains the meaning. Catholic churches are not strictly prohibited in that country.

A man takes off his hat when paying a visit. Both he and

his host extend their right hands and greet each other. They then sit on chairs.

There are no baths in that country like those in Japan, but they use a bath tub. A patient is put into a steam bath and perspiration cures him. Payment for doctors is according to the medicine he gives, not like in Japan where a payment is made twice a year. In some illnesses doctors take blood from the arm. Vaccination is practiced. For smallpox the curing method is to dig out the sores. By this treatment no life is lost.

Toilets are placed over holes in the ground. It is customary to read books in them.

Dwelling houses have glass *shoji* (windows and doors). They have woolen carpets. To make woolen textiles they use sheep's wool. There are machines for making this which do not require human labor. Both machines and lumber saws work automatically.

If a man wishes to get married he looks at a girl and if she is all right the parents on both sides are consulted. There is no exchange of symbolic gifts. If they agree they go to a church and the priest asks, "Do you take this man for your husband, and do you take this woman for your wife?" They then make a promise before God. After they return home there is no celebration but the man takes the girl on an excursion.

Man and wife are very loving and families are peaceful and affectionate. The happiness of their homes is not matched in other countries.

Americans use pianos, fiddles and cellos for musical instruments. They like to sing and often do this when walking along the roads.

The mouth of the port of Fairhaven is fortified with ten guns whose shells are about ten inches in diameter. The guns measure some twelve feet.

The holiday in that country is called the Fourth of July. Fairhaven and New Bedford have warehouses where great number of bayonets are stored. On the holiday men bearing fixed bayonets parade the streets accompanied by musical bands playing such instruments as drums, pipes and gongs. Blank shots are fired. The people go out to see the spectacle and every house entertains guests at dinner. Towards evening the weapons are again put in the store houses.

George Washington is a great hero. He would not tell a lie, even when it was discovered he had cut down a cherry tree.

A piece of gold in that country is worth ten pieces of silver. A piece of silver is equal to one hundred pieces of copper coins. These are called cents. There is also paper money in the United States which is five by three inches.

Women do not use paint or powder on their faces but their natural beauty is great. As a rule they are gentle and chaste.

When they do not have enough to feed their babies they supplement their milk with cow's milk instead of rice.

Sugar is produced from trees by cutting the trunks. When sweet juice comes out they collect it and then boil and condense it.

Casks are made of hard wood and hoops of iron.

When a fire occurs they use a pump to extinguish it.

There are shops which sell cows, sheep, pigs and many kinds of birds.

Horses and pigs are often castrated to make them gentle and fat.

In America there is no bamboo. Elephants, parrots and peacocks come from other countries.

Ordinary men carry watches. When walking they carry canes inside of which swords are often hidden.

Mr. is an honorific title used in place of *San*.

There is no lacquer but containers are made of glass and tin. Lanterns have wicks made of cotton thread.

Shops are surrounded by glass in which they display things for sale. They are very splendid to look at.

Eggs, oil and salt mixed with flour is good food. They call it bread.

Whaling ship expenses are borne by several people. A measurement of whale oil sells for one piece of silver. To attack a whale a ship's boat has three crew members. They carry two harpoons. Parts of the meat which do not contain oil are thrown away. From sperm whales oil is collected from the heads. Ambergris is sometimes collected from the sea and makes high class perfume. Ships are well equipped, even to having a machine to tell how many miles they travel.

It costs about 30,000 pieces of silver to build a whaler and generally it takes about a year to complete.

They spread fish over the grounds for fertilizer. When it decays it is turned into the ground. Farmers sow wheat from the backs of horses because the fields are so large. Tree branches are then used to cover the seed. Vegetables are the same as ours but there is no rice. This comes from China. To harvest wheat they cut it with scythes having long handles. After they cut the wheat they gather it with rakes. Farmers in America sell their wheat at so much per bushel. It is put in cloth bags.

V. YOSHIDA TORAJIRO

With Manjiro's experiences abroad as a spur, and the sympathetic help of his teacher, the celebrated Sakuma Shozan, Yoshida twice attempted to board one of Perry's ships but was repulsed. The account of the first meeting of Perry's offi-

cers with Yoshida and his companion in adventure,
and the commodore's attempts to aid them when
they were found to be in trouble with the authori-
ties, is abbreviated from the official Perry report:

[Officers on shore] had passed into the country beyond
the suburbs [at Shimoda] when they found two Japanese
following them. But, as they were supposed to be a couple
of spies on the watch, little notice was at first taken of them.
Observing, however, that they seemed to be approaching
as though desirous of seeking an opportunity of speaking,
the American officers awaited their coming up.

Their manners showed the usual courtly refinement of
the better classes, but they exhibited the embarrassment
of men who evidently were not perfectly at their ease, and
were about to do something of dubious propriety. They
cast their eyes stealthily about, as if to assure themselves
that none of their countrymen were at hand to observe their
proceedings, and then approaching one of the officers and
pretending to admire his watch chain, slipped within the
breast of his coat a folded paper. [It proved to be a letter.]
They now, with fingers on their lips, rapidly made off.

During the succeeding night about two o'clock A.M., the
officer on mid-watch was aroused by a voice from a boat
alongside, and upon proceeding to the gangway, found a
couple of Japanese who had mounted the ladder at the
ship's side. Upon being accosted, they made signs expressive
of a desire to be admitted on board.

They seemed very eager to be allowed to remain. The
captain of the *Mississippi* directed them to the flag-ship,
and retiring to their boat, they pulled off at once. They
reached the ship with some difficulty because of a heavy
swell in the harbor. Hardly had they got upon the ladder
and mounted to the gangway, when their boat got adrift,
either by accident, or from being let go intentionally. The

officer on watch informed the Commodore of their presence, and he sent his interpreter to learn the purpose of
their untimely visit. They frankly confessed that their object was to be taken to the United States. They were now
recognized as the two men who had met the officers on
shore, and given one of them the letter. They seemed much
fatigued by their efforts and their clothes showed signs of
being travel worn, although they proved to be Japanese
gentlemen of good position. [Yoshida's companion was
actually a common foot soldier who had become a student
follower, called a disciple, and was not of samurai rank.]

The Commodore, on learning the purpose of their visit,
sent word that he regretted that he was unable to receive
them, as he would like very much to take some Japanese to
America with him. He, however, was compelled to refuse
them until they had received permission from their government. For this they would have ample opportunity, as the
squadron would remain in the harbor of Shimoda for some
time longer. They were greatly disturbed by this answer,
and declaring that they would lose their heads if they
returned to the land, earnestly implored to be allowed to
remain. A long discussion followed, in the course of which
they offered every possible argument in their favor, and
continued to appeal to the humanity of the Americans. A
boat was now lowered, and they descended the gangway
piteously deploring their fate. They were landed at a spot
near where it was supposed their boat might have drifted.

On the afternoon of the next day, Yenosuke, the chief
interpreter, came on board the *Powhatan,* and requesting
to see the flag-lieutenant, stated that last night a couple of
demented Japanese had gone off to one of the American
vessels. They wished to know if it was the flag-ship; and if
so, whether the men had been guilty of any impropriety.
The flag-lieutenant replied that it was difficult to retain any
precise recollection of those constantly coming and going

from the shore in the watering boats and on other business, but he assured the interpreter that no misdemeanor could have been committed, or he would have been aware of the fact. The interpreter then asked whether the Japanese referred to had reached the shore in safety, and was told that they had.

The Commodore, upon hearing of the apparent anxiety of the Japanese authorities, sent an officer on shore in order to quiet the excitement which had been created, and to interpose as far as possible in behalf of the poor fellows, who, it was certain, would be pursued with the utmost rigor of the Japanese law. The authorities were thanked for the solicitude they had expressed and assured that they need not trouble themselves for a moment with the thought that so slight a matter had been considered worthy of any investigation. The Japanese were further informed that they need give themselves no anxiety for the future, as none of their countrymen would be received on board the American ships without the consent of the authorities. They were further informed that the Commodore was not disposed to take advantage of their confidence or to act in any way that would be inconsistent with the spirit of the treaty.

Some days later as a party of officers was strolling in the suburbs they came upon the prison of the town where they recognized the two unfortunate Japanese in a kind of cage, barred in front and very restricted in dimensions. The poor fellows had been immediately pursued and after a few days were caught. They seemed to bear their misfortune with great equanimity, and were greatly pleased with the visit of the American officers, in whose eyes they were evidently desirous of appearing to advantage. One of the officers approached the cage and received a note written on a piece of board. The final words were: "How can we find an exit from this place? Weeping, we seem as fools; laughing as rogues. Alas for us! Silent we can only be."

When the Commodore was informed of the imprisoned Japanese he sent his flag-lieutenant on shore to ascertain unofficially whether they were the same two who had visited the ships. The cage was found as described, but empty, and the guards declared that the men had been sent that morning to Yedo in obedience to a higher order.

The fate of the poor fellows was never ascertained, but it is hoped that the authorities were more merciful than to have inflicted the severest penalty, which was the loss of their heads, for what appeared to us only highly commendable curiosity. It is a comfort to be able to add that the Commodore received assurances from the authorities that he need not apprehend a serious termination.

[History reveals that after long imprisonment, during which his companion died, Yoshida became involved in a conspiracy against the Shogunate. He was executed at the age of twenty-nine, a martyr to the New Japan.]

VI. SAM PATCH

(Abbreviated from the Perry Report)

Sentaro, dubbed Sam Patch by the sailors, was one of the crew consisting of sixteen men of a Japanese junk which had been driven off in a storm from the coast of Japan. An American merchant vessel, having fallen in with the junk, took the Japanese on board and conveyed them to San Francisco, where they were removed to a revenue cutter. They remained on the cutter twelve months, when they were taken by the United States sloop-of-war *St. Mary's* to China, and there transferred to the *Susquehanna*. When this steamer joined the squadron, bound for Japan, the Japanese preferred to remain in China, lest if they return home they should lose their lives. The one exception was Sam Patch, who remained on board, and being regularly shipped as one of the crew, was with the squadron on the first, as he was again on the second visit to Japan.

According to agreement, Sam Patch was brought forward and presented to the Japanese officials, but no sooner did he behold these dignitaries than he prostrated himself, apparently completely awe-stricken. Sam had so frequently been laughed at during the voyage by his messmates, and teased by statements of the danger to which his head would be exposed on arrival in his own country, that the poor fellow possibly thought that his last hour had come. Seeing him crouching in the most abject fear, and trembling in every limb, Captain Adams ordered him to rise. He was reminded that he was on board an American man-of-war, as perfectly safe as one of her crew. It being impossible to reassure him while in the presence of his countrymen, he was soon dismissed.

A few days previous to the departure of the Commodore, Moriyama Yenosuke, the Japanese interpreter, in company with several other officials, came on board the *Powhatan* to request that the Japanese "Sam Patch" should be allowed to remain in Japan. They were told that the Commodore had no objection whatever to the man's remaining, if he wished; but that it must be done by his own free will, and that the commissioners must give a written pledge that the man should not, in any way, be punished for his absence from Japan. Moreover, as he suffered shipwreck, and had been thrown, by God's providence, on American protection, he was entitled to all the security of an American citizen; consequently the Commodore could allow of no coercion being resorted to to make the man remain in Japan. The Japanese officials ridiculed the idea of his suffering any harm by remaining in Japan, and said that the commissioners would cheerfully give any guarantee that he should in no way be molested. He would, they stated, be allowed to return to his friends, who were very anxious to see him.

Sam was now called up, but all the eloquence and persuasiveness of the Japanese were insufficient to induce him to leave the ship. The truth is that Sam never, during the whole stay of the squadron in Japan, appeared fully to understand the independence and safety of his position. Long habit had so impressed upon him the need of trembling servility before his Japanese superiors, that it was very obvious the contact produced no emotion but abject fear. He had won the goodwill of his shipmates by his good nature. All pitied him, and one of the marines named Goble had begun a system of instruction which he hoped would not only make the Japanese a fair English scholar, but a faithful Christian. Sam came to the United States on the *Mississippi,* and accompanied his benevolent shipmate to his home in New York. At last accounts they were living there together, and it is not unreasonable to hope that Sam may yet be instrumental in the introduction to Japan of a higher and better civilization. All honor to the Christian marine for his benevolence!

Mr. Damon recorded in *The Friend* of March 1, 1860, that "Sam Patch" was in Honolulu with his benefactor, Mr. J. Goble, who had become a Baptist missionary. They were returning to Japan with the expectation of carrying forward a missionary enterprise. That Sam never became a strong influence in his own country is attested by the historian, W. E. Griffis, who in 1872 saw him at the home of E. Warren Clark, an early American teacher stationed at Shidzuoka. He was employed as a servant and appeared unable to rise above that status. "Sammy's notoriety," commented Griffis, "has somewhat spoiled his pristine modesty, and his head, having never been ballasted with over two-thirds of the average quantum of wit, is occasionally turned."

The sobriquet, Sam Patch, marks his grave in a temple cemetery at Oji, near Tokyo.

Index

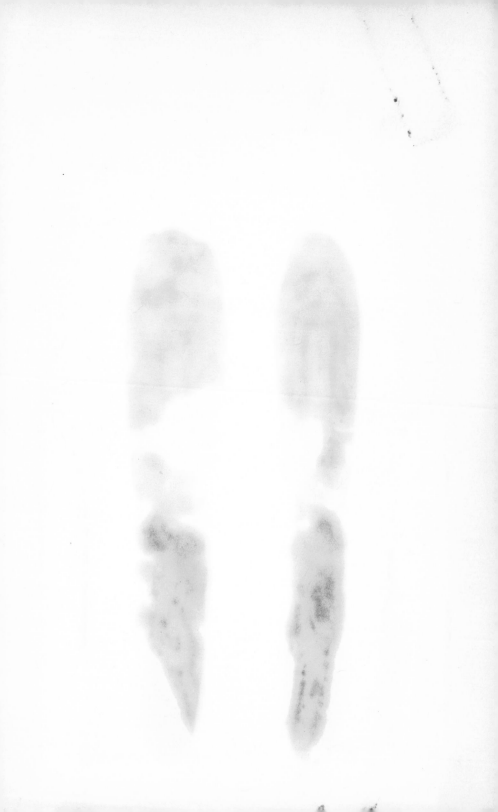